The No Baloney Sandwich Book

by Alden Robertson

illustrated by his brother

A Dolphin Book
Doubleday & Company, Inc.
Garden City, New York 1978

Printed in the United States of America
Library of Congress Catalog Card Number 77-80145
ISBN 0-385-12429-5

This book was edited and prepared for publication
at The Yolla Bolly Press, Covelo, California.
The work was done between February and June 1977
under the supervision of James and Carolyn Robertson.
Production staff: Gene Floyd, Loren Fisher,
Jay Stewart, Joyca Cunnan, Michael Ludwig.

To sweet Jean
who gave me a weekly allowance
while I wrote this book
and who helped in other ways.

Contents

Madison Avenue Makes Lousy Sandwiches

There was once an English nobleman named John Montagu, the Fourth Earl of Sandwich, who was a very enthusiastic gambler. As a matter of fact, Lord Sandwich must have been a real nut about gambling; on at least one occasion he became so involved in whatever game he was playing, he wouldn't even stop to eat. History has failed to record exactly what happened, but evidently our hero ended up clutching his cards in one hand and a "sandwich" in the other. I don't imagine his companions were terribly impressed with the Earl's antics, but they had no way of knowing how significant the meal he was enjoying would turn out to be. Neither, I am sure, did the Earl, as he sat there spilling crumbs all over himself and the green felt-covered table.

I assume that a sandwich, eaten about 200 years ago, was both simple and good. Most likely it was nothing more than two slices of bread with a chunk of mutton or beef in between. The bread must have been pretty good, because in those days the flour did not have the whole grain refined out of it. There's a good chance the meat was also quite palatable for more or less the same reason; it had not been tampered with. The most important thing about that sandwich, however, was the reason for its invention. It was a meal easily prepared and eaten.

For the same reason, sandwiches are one of the most frequently eaten items on the American menu. Unfortunately, the very fact of their popularity has been their downfall. Look at the state of the art of preparing a sandwich: take one slice of processed meat or cheese and slap it between two slices of squishy, white bread. That's it. An extraordinarily elaborate sandwich might contain both meat and cheese with a wisp of mustard or sandwich spread smeared across one of the slices of bread. Wrapped in a plastic bag, it is then ready to be carried about until later in the day when it will be dutifully eaten with little, if any, enjoyment.

I don't mean to suggest that a good sandwich requires a great amount of time in preparation or that the best sandwiches are the most elaborate. What I am suggesting is that the products provided specifically for making sandwiches generally reflect a good deal of consideration for convenient use and little else. We are buying craftily designed, prepackaged, sliced, sandwich-sized, processed meat and cheese, spreads and breads — not because they are especially good or even cheap, but because they are easy to

The Fourth Earl of Sandwich and
friends at the gaming table

use. Always in a hurry, we have fallen easy prey to the wizardry of Madison Avenue. On behalf of the industry that created the monster of processed foods, they almost have us convinced that our inventiveness in sandwich making must be limited to using only those packaged products we find in the delicatessen section of the local supermarket.

A definition here will give you some idea of your alternatives. A sandwich is simply two slices of bread with any edible ingredient used as a filling in between. And while the simplicity of this description does little to whet the appetite, it is the basis for the anything-goes approach to sandwich making that this book is all about. I am unable to think of any reason why a sandwich cannot be made out of whatever strikes your fancy. The Earl had meat in his sandwich, but if I want parsnips in mine, then that's all right too. The list of ingredients suitable for making sandwiches is practically endless, and of course includes those supermarket deli items previously mentioned. The point is, there are many, many choices on the list; some choices, perhaps less obvious than others, will in fact make better sandwiches. This book explores these alternatives.

Sandwiches can be as imaginative and elaborate as you want to make them, or as quick and as simple. There is no reason why they should not all be delicious. We are free to devise mind-boggling concoctions which will provide as exquisite and varied a taste treat as any other food. In support of this premise, I offer you an orgy of sandwiches, from the simple and traditional to the most palatably exotic imaginable. You have at your fingertips an ambrosial wealth of possibilities. Enjoy them.

What You Should Know About Sandwiches

What You Should Know About Sandwiches

For our purposes, a sandwich consists of four parts: the covering, the filling, the garnish, and the relish.

The covering is the thing that made the first sandwich an innovation because it enabled a person to pick up and eat out-of-hand, anywhere, what he or she previously had to eat in a more formal manner at a table. As far as I am concerned, it doesn't matter exactly what variation of covering is used, as long as it is good substantial breadstuff and not some bleached white fluff. There are many good breads available these days, of which rye and the whole grained varieties are two examples. Actually, the covering needn't even be slices of bread, but could be a roll or English muffin instead.

What you use, of course, depends upon what is available and that depends upon where you live: San Francisco has sourdough French bread and rolls; Tacoma, Washington, is where Roman Meal bread originated; and in El Paso, Texas, you can find a wonderful, semisweet roll called a *bolillo*. Wherever you live, you are apt to find some good, indigenous breads, rolls, buns, or muffins with which to cover the insides of your sandwiches. By all means, use them.

In this book, recipes will most often call for a particular bread, but sometimes the choice is yours. On the occasions that I recommend a bread, it will be chosen from those for which I give the recipes in the following chapter. If you have neither the time nor the inclination to make your own bread, you should try buying a local bread that comes the closest to the one recommended. (Please keep in mind my disdainful remarks regarding squishy white bread, which is little different from squishy wheat bread.) On the other hand, if a recipe calls for a bread you do not have or cannot get, don't worry about it. Use what you have or substitute what you can get. Still, whenever it's possible and practical, try the bread the recipe calls for. Fresh, homemade bread is the best.

The filling is what a sandwich is named after, as in parsnip sandwich. If you dare to eat it, chances are you can make a sandwich out of it. A filling is prepared in any of three ways: as a salad, as a spread, or in chunks. In a salad filling, chicken salad for example, the chicken is chopped up and mixed with another ingredient, mayonnaise for instance. Spreads tend to be less moist and gooey and more pasty than salad fillings, and the main ingredient is visibly less recognizable. There are many possibilities for spreads, but the most famous is peanut butter. Or is it jam? By chunks I mean that the main ingredient is in large pieces or slices, as in a ham or ham and cheese sandwich.

Whatever the filling, it will generally require seasoning, if only a little salt and pepper. But don't hesitate to use something as esoteric as fresh coriander if that's what you think it needs or a recipe calls for it. You should know that Spice Islands is now bottling coriander leaves, also called cilantro. It is not nearly as flavorful dried as

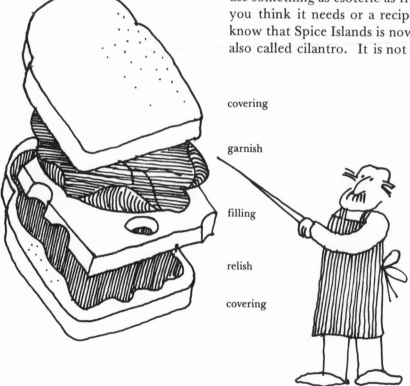

covering

garnish

filling

relish

covering

when it is fresh. Cilantro is very easy to grow in your garden (or in a window box) as are many herbs you're apt to use.

You're liable to use just as many herbs and spices making sandwiches as you are in preparing any other food. If your spice shelf looks rather meager, you should think about adding to your collection. I prefer Spice Island products to any other and, for the most part, whole herbs to ground. I use a lot of whole dried thyme, marjoram, and oregano; also coarse ground black pepper, and ground paprika and cayenne. Fresh basil, rosemary, cilantro, and parsley we grow in our garden. I often use curry powder and ginger. Use fresh ginger root, grated, if you can get it. If not, you will have to use ground ginger. Do try growing some of your own herbs.

The garnish along with the relish is a frequently neglected part of a sandwich. Lettuce is the most commonly used garnish, but any other vegetable, or even fruit, will do. I like red lettuce, but it is fragile and wilts in the sandwich if not eaten within a short period of time. My next choice, butter lettuce, is most people's first choice. It is a little more hearty than red lettuce, but still less so than iceberg or romaine. One alternative to lettuce is spinach — fresh, of course. It is as hearty as any lettuce, and if it does happen to wilt a bit, it is not as bad as wilted lettuce. Perhaps the best garnish of all is alfalfa sprouts. They are always fresh, and will remain so, even in the sandwich, because they are always growing. For more information about growing sprouts, see page 96.

If you generally make sandwiches to be eaten later in the day, at lunch for instance, be sure to use a hearty lettuce, spinach, or alfalfa sprouts. Keep in mind that the runnier the filling, the more apt the garnish is to wilt. You might also consider packing some parts of the sandwich separately, to be assembled just before eating, though personally, I think this is a real bother and wouldn't do it.

The relish need not be sweet, as in hot dog relish, but it could be. It could also be mustard and mayonnaise or something you yourself invent. My favorite brand of mayonnaise is Best Foods. All the others I have tried become somewhat separated and a little runny. Also, Best Foods tastes the best. If it is not available, hopefully

Hellmann's will be. It is the same mayonnaise with a different name. If you have the time, make your own mayonnaise. There is a recipe on page 44. Whether homemade or store bought, be sure to keep it refrigerated.

A good, general purpose mustard would be one of the types which originated in Dijon, France. This mustard is made with white wine and is fairly mild but very tasty. I have found the most readily available brand of Dijon-style mustard is Grey Poupon, made by Heublein. There are other kinds of mustard — English, German, and Chinese for example. Some are hot, and others less so. I would not suggest using American-style, prepared mustard on anything except hot dogs. Please turn to page 82 for a mustard recipe.

The important thing to remember about both the garnish and relish is that they not only contribute to the flavor of the sandwich, but are also a source of often badly needed moisture. A dry sandwich is, at best, unpleasant to chew and difficult to swallow — in a word — awful. The addition of nothing more than a little lettuce and mayonnaise can make the same sandwich exquisitely palatable.

The whole idea of this book is to work a little imagination and excitement into your sandwich making. So if you don't have a particular ingredient, leave it out, unless you're sure that will ruin the sandwich. Better yet, improvise. Try a substitute ingredient or change a whole recipe around to suit yourself and the ingredients you have available. Whatever you do, it will most likely turn out just fine.

Making Bread

Making Bread

Because bread is such an important part of a good sandwich, and because good bread might not be available to everyone, you are here provided with a small selection of recipes and some simple instructions in the mechanics of making bread. If you are already an accomplished breadmaker, then you certainly need not concern yourself with my instructions. But you should try some of the recipes; they are excellent. If you have never made bread before, be encouraged. You can do it! In fact, I think you will find it the most satisfying thing you have done, or ever will do, in your kitchen.

I have provided six bread recipes. The Swedish rye recipe was contributed by my mother, the herb bread by a friend who owns a little restaurant where I live in Point Richmond, California, called Judges and Spares, and all the rest — the egg bread, the cheese bread, the oat-sesame bread, and the orange-raisin bread — were contributed by the friendly bakers at my favorite bread and cheese store, Say Cheese, in Berkeley. All the recipes have been changed to some extent, and I had to reduce all but the Swedish rye recipe from the original 16- to 20-loaf batches to the present 2 loaves. I will be very pleased if all those who provided me with recipes still want to lay claim to their contributions.

I will first discuss my breadmaking method in general terms. For the time being, don't worry about quantities and details, just the process. It begins with the combination of three groups of ingredients.

The first group consists of yeast, water, sweetener, maybe powdered milk, maybe an egg or two, and enough flour to thicken the mixture to a consistency you can just stir with a spoon. It is mixed in a 6- to 8-quart bowl.

Stir it until your arm aches, then stir some more. When it is perfectly smooth, stop and put the bowl aside for 15 or 20 minutes. I am not sure if this mixture qualifies as a sponge, a term used by breadmakers, but that is what I will call it. The idea of the sponge is to give the yeast a running start in the company of helpful ingredients, or at least without those that might hinder its work.

The next group of ingredients is generally those requiring some preparation, such as cooking, grating, or chopping, and so on. You can be preparing these items (whole grains, carrots, nuts, etc.) while the sponge is working. When the yeast has gotten a good start in its short life, this second group of ingredients is folded — rather than stirred — into the sponge.

The last group of ingredients (salt, oil, flour, etc.) is combined with the rest, again by folding in the ingredients. I pour them on top of the sponge and fold the sponge over them from one side to the other until all are combined. The folding-in part is very discouraging because you have taken your beautiful, pristine sponge and dumped all this junk on top, and then, to complete its ruin, tried to mix everything together. The worst thing is that nothing seems to combine and it looks as though it never will. Do not despair! It will be even worse if you plop this mess onto the breadboard before it is ready. You will be scraping sticky dough off your hands and the board for the next hour.

When the dough stops, or nearly stops, sticking to the side of the bowl, it is ready to go on the breadboard for kneading. The dough will still be slightly sticky and there will still probably be flour left to add. That is used on the board and on your hands. If you have managed to fold in all the flour called for in the recipe, then simply use some extra to keep the dough from sticking to everything. White flour is most effective for this. I like to knead at least 10 minutes and sometimes as many as 15 or 20 minutes depending upon how the dough looks and feels. I also enjoy it. I flatten the lump of dough with the heels of my hands, give it a quarter turn, fold it in half toward me, and start over again — pushing and twisting first on the near side until the fold is stuck together; then I work my way toward the rear, pushing and twisting, always with the heels of the hands, quarter turn, fold, and start over again. Just be careful that in the process of kneading, you don't add so much flour that the dough dries out, and the folds can't be made to stick together. What you are doing with all this kneading is continuing to combine the ingredients and you want to do as thorough a job of this as possible. As the dough is kneaded, you will see everything sort of smooth out, unless, of course, some ingredients are lumpy, like seeds and nuts. But even then you will be able to tell when it's ready because the dough will smooth out around the expected lumps. More important, the dough will develop a wonderful elasticity or springiness. What you cannot see is a whole chain of magical events taking place in that lump of dough beneath your hands. A substance called gluten is absorbing the moisture you have provided and through your

kneading, forming an elastic structural system throughout the dough. Already the yeast, living single-celled organisms, literally billions of them, has begun to feed on a sugar derived from the starch in the flour, and a gas called carbon dioxide is thus formed which swells the dough and tests the strength of the gluten structure. Once you stop kneading, the dough will ever so slowly begin to rise, increasing its size until it has doubled or even tripled its original dimensions. Yaaahoo! I love making bread!

When the kneading is finished, form the dough into a shape which will sit comfortably in your mixing bowl, now cleaned and oiled. Cover the bowl with a damp cloth so the dough inside will not dry out and place the bowl in a warm spot to rise for 45 minutes to 1 hour or until it has doubled its size. Then while it is still in the bowl, punch it down with your fist by pushing down the risen dough a number of times until it has completely collapsed and no longer yields.

Although the only recipe in this chapter that calls for a second rising is the egg bread, if you prefer a little lighter loaf, you might want to take the time for a second, shorter rising with some of the others as well.

Now cut the dough in half and prepare the bread pans by oiling them. I use lots of butter for this which makes a nice rich bottom crust. Any good heavy pan, glass or steel, that conducts heat evenly will work. Take one of the halves of the dough and with the heel of one hand knead it, meanwhile you keep folding it in half and turning it with the other hand. Do this until you feel the dough begin to tighten and become so springy that it is difficult to flatten. As when kneading previously, you are dealing with the strength of the gluten structure, winding it up like a coiled spring. At this point, flatten out the dough enough to fold or roll it into a cylinder about the length of the bread pan and pinch the seam closed. Put it into the pan, seam down, and with the backs of your fingers push down to flatten it somewhat and fill the pan from corner to corner.

Do the same with the other half and set both pans in a warm place and let the loaves rise for about 20 or 30 minutes. You need not cover them this time.

When ready to bake, turn the oven on to 350 degrees and while it is heating up, use a razor blade to ventilate the top of each loaf. I make one slit, lengthwise down the center of the loaf. The last thing I do is an egg wash. It is simply 1 beaten egg mixed with 1/4 cup of water and brushed on the top of the loaf. It gives the crust a dark, glazed look and makes it harder than it would otherwise be. Next, if you wish, you can sprinkle some seeds or nuts on the top.

You are now ready to bake, which at 350 degrees will take about 45 minutes. At least you should check your loaves at that time. Just dump them out of the pans and holding one upside down with one hand, slap its bottom with the other. If it sounds hollow and resonant, the loaves are ready and should be placed on a wire rack to cool. If the loaf makes a dull thump when slapped, then they should both go back in the oven *sans* pans, for another 5 or 10 minutes.

When you are done, be sure to eat some with lots of butter while it's still warm. Mmmmm! Delicious!

Now you know everything I do about making bread, and while that is not exactly a great store of knowledge considering what there is to know, it is enough to enable us to make some very good breads. However, if you are anxious to learn even more, then there is a book I would like to recommend to you. It is *The Tassajara Bread Book* written by Edward Espe Brown and published by Shambala Publications, now in Boulder, Colorado.

The first recipe, for egg bread, is extensive in its explanation. In fact, for the benefit of those who refuse to read anything in cookbooks except the recipes, I have repeated some of the previous instructions. In subsequent recipes it may be necessary to refer back to the general instructions or the egg-bread recipe if you cannot remember a part of the procedure.

Slicing the Daily Loaf

Day one and two: bread for
    sandwiches
Day three: bread for toast
Day four: bread for bread pudding
    or French toast
Day five: bread for croutons or
    bird food

Day one and two | Day three | Day four | Day five

A rich, light white bread.

EGG BREAD

1 1/2 cups warm water
2 tablespoons yeast
1/2 cup sugar
3/4 cup dried milk
3 eggs
1 1/2 cups gluten flour
2 cups unbleached white flour

1 1/3 tablespoons salt
1/3 cup corn oil
3 cups unbleached white flour

In a 6- to 8-quart mixing bowl thoroughly dissolve the yeast in the warm water (100 degrees maximum), then add the sugar and dried milk. Beat the eggs and then add them to the mixture, stirring with a whisk until all the dried ingredients have dissolved and there are no more lumps. Now add the gluten and white flour and stir again for all you are worth, this time with a wooden spoon. The longer you are able to stir the better, but 5 minutes should be enough. When the sponge has become very smooth and also very sticky, it is ready to be set aside, still in the bowl, for 15 or 20 minutes. You can let it rise for as much as an hour, but in that case, you should cover it with a damp cloth.

After the appropriate length of time, fold in the remaining ingredients. To do this, pour the oil, salt, and 1 cup of flour over the top of the sponge, then push the spoon down the side of the bowl under the sponge and fold the sponge over the top of these ingredients. Each time you fold over the sponge, turn the bowl a little and start at a different spot. Keep adding flour and folding it in until you think the dough is the proper consistency for kneading. You will have used more or less the amount of flour called for in the recipe.

When kneading use a bit more flour to keep the dough from sticking to everything. Knead for at least 10 minutes, longer if the dough looks and feels as though it needs it. If it begins to dry out, stop kneading.

When you are finished, return the dough to the mixing bowl, now cleaned and oiled, and set in a warm place

---

Buying Ingredients for Bread

The ingredients used in making bread are most often available in natural food stores and are generally in bulk form. You will have to get at least some items in a natural food store since they are not apt to be available elsewhere, so you might as well buy all your breadmaking supplies at the same time. A bulk item will always be cheaper than its packaged counterpart and there is seldom, if ever, any reason to question the quality of these items.

Gluten flour, a white flour with a high gluten content, is one of the products I have only found in natural food stores. Another such item is baker's yeast in bulk. This yeast seems to be considerably more active than either yeast cakes or packaged, dry yeast. I buy enough to fill a quart jar and store it, tightly sealed, in the refrigerator. There are two different types of dry milk available these days. One is the granular, instant variety found in most grocery stores. I do not suggest using this product. The other type is a fine powder, difficult to mix but it is far richer than instant dry milk. It is available in natural food stores in bulk and is what I use in making bread. Because it contains a considerable amount of milk fat, it must be stored in a sealed container in the refrigerator or it will turn rancid.

If, for some reason, I find it necessary to buy packaged flour at a grocery store, I always buy Stone-Buhr flour, milled by the Stone-Buhr Milling Co. in Seattle, Washington. Their whole wheat flour is stone ground and has a wonderful, coarse texture. It is expensive but an excellent product and worth the cost. Aside from the standard ingredients like eggs and sugar, this flour is the only breadmaking ingredient I am apt to buy anyplace other than a natural food store.

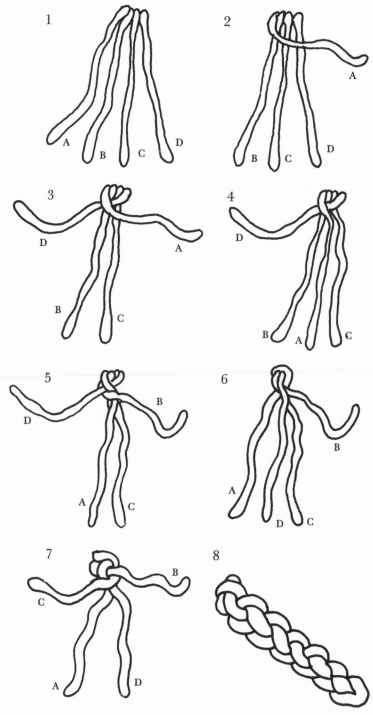

How to braid 4 strands
(after Edward Espe Brown, *The Tassajara Bread Book*).

(85 to 100 degrees) for about an hour or until the dough has doubled its size. When the first rise is complete, punch the dough down and allow it to rise once more. It will take less time to double its size during the second rise. After about 45 minutes dump the dough out on the breadboard to be cut into loaves. At this point you have a choice of making egg bread or cheese bread, which is simply egg bread in a different shape and filled with cheese. There is enough dough to make two large braided loaves of egg bread, or four smaller cheese bread loaves, or one braided egg bread loaf and two cheese bread loaves. If you want to make cheese bread, please turn to the next recipe. The following instructions apply to the braided egg bread loaves (2).

Divide the dough in half and set one half aside. Divide the other half into 4 equal parts and, using your hands, roll and stretch each of these until they are 16 or 18 inches long. Braid these 4 strands. If the result looks attractive, and doesn't unwind in the oven, that is all that matters. Repeat this procedure for the other half of the dough and set the 2 loaves on an oiled cookie sheet to rise for about 20 minutes. You can also stuff these braided loaves into a bread pan, in which case you should make the strands a little shorter and allow lots of head room in the oven, because it will be a very tall loaf. In fact you might have to make 3 loaves instead of just 2.

After the loaves have risen, and while the oven is heating up to 350 degrees, brush on a light egg wash and sprinkle a few sesame or poppy seeds on top. If you bake the bread on a cookie sheet, it will take about 35 minutes; but allow a little more time if the loaves are in bread pans.

Italian Herbs

1 part each:

Marjoram
Rosemary
Basil
Thyme
Savory

1/2 part:

Sage

Not really a sandwich bread, but too good to leave out.

CHEESE BREAD

Egg bread dough (see preceding
   recipe)
1 pound sharp Cheddar cheese
1 teaspoon Italian herbs (see box)
1/4 teaspoon dill weed
1/2 teaspoon dill seed
1/2 teaspoon garlic powder
1/2 teaspoon coarse ground black
   pepper
1/2 teaspoon salt

Grate the cheese while it is cold and mix in the seasonings.

After the egg bread dough has risen in the bowl for the second time, dump it out on the breadboard and cut it into 4 equal parts. This will make 4 loaves. Cut each of these 4 parts in half, then roll out the 2 halves flat with a rolling pin. With a large mixing spoon, scoop up a heaping spoonful of the seasoned cheese and lay it down the center of each of the 8 flattened-out portions of dough. Use up all of the seasoned cheese. Now fold the dough around the cheese and pinch the seam closed, sealing everything inside. Twist 2 of these strands around one another and then loop the whole thing so the ends just cross to form a twisted and more or less circular loaf. Pinch all the ends together and fold them under the loaf. Repeat the process for the other 3 loaves.

Place the loaves on an oiled cookie sheet and allow to rise for 30 minutes. If you do not give them enough time to rise at this point, they are apt to rise too quickly in the oven and burst, letting all the cheese run out. Preheat the oven to 350 degrees and after a light egg wash, bake the loaves for no more than 40 minutes. Check them prior to that time because you often cannot trust your oven temperature. Rely on your eyes instead.

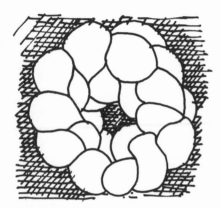

Your formed loaf will look something like this

A heavy-duty moist, chewy whole wheat bread.

OAT-SESAME BREAD

2 cups boiling water
1 1/4 cups rolled oats
1 1/4 cups warm water
2 tablespoons yeast
1/3 cup honey
1/3 cup dark molasses
3 1/2 cups whole wheat flour
1 tablespoon salt
1/4 cup corn oil
2/3 cup sesame seeds, toasted
3 cups whole wheat flour

Cook the oats for 10 minutes, then let them cool. Dissolve the yeast in warm water, add the honey and molasses, and stir. If the oats have not yet cooled, throw in a couple of ice cubes and stir them around until they have melted and the oats are just barely warm. Now mix the oats in with the water, yeast, and molasses, and add the flour. Stir out all the lumps and set aside for 20 minutes.

While the sponge is working, toast the sesame seeds. Then, when the sponge is ready, fold in the seeds and remaining ingredients. Knead the heck out of it and set it in a warm place to rise, in a bowl covered with a damp cloth. It will probably take the dough an hour, maybe longer, to double its size.

After one rise, divide the dough into 2 portions and wind up each one with a little additional kneading until it becomes springy. Then roll the 2 pieces, pinch the seams closed, and put them into oiled or buttered bread pans. Let the loaves rise in the pans for 30 minutes or so. Unlike white bread, these loaves won't rise much in the oven, so give them plenty of time to rise beforehand. While the oven is heating up to 350 degrees, ventilate the top of the loaves with some slits and, if you like, apply an egg wash. Bake for 45 or 50 minutes.

What Do You Do When the Dough Don't Rise, or How to Make Unleavened Bread

The first thing I generally do is go berserk. I shout a lot and maybe slam a few doors or shout at my wife if she's around. Whatever you do though, don't throw away the dough.

It once took 4 hours at about 100 degrees for a batch of egg bread dough to rise the first time, and another 3 hours for the second rise. The cloth covering the bowl had to be kept damp that whole time to prevent the dough from forming a crust. I also used an atomizer to spray a light mist directly on the dough.

So first, make sure it is not going to rise. Once you are convinced, just consider it an unyeasted bread and proceed accordingly. If you are lucky, it will be one of the grainy breads because so are the traditional unyeasted breads. If it is a white flour bread like the egg bread, then I am afraid you might as well give it to your children to make dough sculptures and then bake those.

We will assume you are lucky and it is a suitably grainy dough, in which case simply divide it into loaves and, preparing them as you would for any other bread, put them in bread pans. If by this time the dough has been sitting around for 6 or more hours, then give it another hour in the pan before baking. If you prefer, it could also stay in the pan overnight.

Because the dough is so dense, you will have to bake it at a hotter temperature for a longer period of time than you do a yeasted bread. Beyond telling you that, there is little more I can say.

If the bread is edible, you made out. If it is not, you have my sympathy. Your failure will have been honorable because you persevered. In either case, you had better figure out what went wrong with the yeast.

A raisin and everything-else-but-the-kitchen-sink bread. It is still light and not too sweet.

ORANGE-RAISIN BREAD

1 cup warm water
2 tablespoons yeast
1 tablespoon honey
1 egg, beaten
2/3 cup warm orange juice
3 cups unbleached white flour

1 cup seedless raisins
1 1/2 cups grated carrots
1 cup walnut quarters, chopped
2 tablespoons grated orange peel
1/2 teaspoon cinnamon
1/4 teaspoon allspice
1/4 teaspoon nutmeg

2 teaspoons salt
1/4 cup corn oil
1 cup whole wheat flour
2 cups unbleached white flour

Using the first group of ingredients, make a sponge. While that is working, prepare the ingredients in the second group. The carrots should be finely grated. Measure the walnuts as quarters and then chop them up. Fold all of these ingredients into the sponge before you add any of those in the last group.

Knead the dough and let it rise once. Divide the dough in half and prepare the 2 portions for the bread pans. Bake the 2 loaves at 350 degrees for about 45 minutes.

Sort of an egg bread with herbs, it will appeal to all those addicted to dill.

HERB BREAD

2 cups warm water
2 tablespoons yeast
1/3 cup sugar
2 eggs, beaten
1 1/2 cups gluten flour
2 cups unbleached white flour

2 teaspoons salt
1/3 cup corn oil
3 cups unbleached white flour

1 tablespoon dill weed
1 tablespoon dill seed
1 teaspoon anise seed
2 tablespoons dried parsley

Make the sponge first. Measure out the herbs, putting them together in a cup or bowl. You may use fresh parsley if you like, but chop it up finely and use at least triple the amount called for. Fold the herbs into the sponge first and then add in the balance of the ingredients. This bread gets one rise in the bowl and another in the pan, both after kneading, of course. Bake the 2 loaves at 350 degrees for about 40 or 50 minutes.

A grainy but light bread with a hint of orange, as in the style of the Swedes.

RYE BREAD

2 cups warm water
2 tablespoons yeast
1/3 cup dark molasses
1/2 cup dried milk
3 cups unbleached white flour

1/2 cup boiling water
1/2 cup cracked wheat
1 teaspoon fennel seed
1 teaspoon caraway seed
2 teaspoons grated orange peel

2 teaspoons salt
1/3 cup corn oil
2 cups rye meal
1 cup whole wheat flour

When you are mixing a sponge containing dried milk, it will be very lumpy. A whisk is best for stirring out these milk lumps. Instant dried milk will not lump up, but on the other hand it is not as rich, and I do not recommend using it. Of course you have to change to a spoon in order to mix in the flour.

After mixing the sponge, boil the 1/2 cup of water and add the cracked wheat, immediately turning off the heat. After that has cooled and the sponge is ready, fold in all of the ingredients in the second group. Then fold in the balance of the ingredients and knead. This bread rises once in the bowl and once again in the pan. Bake the 2 loaves at 350 degrees for 40 minutes.

While you have been wading through this bread chapter, I hope you have been making more than just breakfast toast with your fresh, homemade bread. Make sandwiches with your good bread, good folks, make sandwiches!

Straight Sandwiches
(In Which There Is Only One Main Ingredient)

This is one of the two best ways I have for dealing with leftover tongue, either beef or lamb. The other is on page 81.

MARINATED TONGUE

1/2 to 1 pound tongue, sliced
1/2 cup olive oil
2 teaspoons dry mustard
1/4 cup lemon juice
1/4 teaspoon coarse ground
   black pepper
1/2 teaspoon salt
1 tablespoon cilantro

First you must make the marinade. Mix the mustard with a little of the olive oil to make a paste, then combine that with the balance of the ingredients. You might want to vary the amount of the marinade depending upon how much meat you have left over. Slice the tongue very thinly and soak in the marinade overnight before refrigerating.

Use the meat to make the following sandwich or one of your own invention. One-half pound will make at least 2 and probably 3 sandwiches.

Sliced, marinated tongue
Horseradish
Mayonnaise
Radishes, sliced
Butter lettuce
Bread of your choice

You may mix the horseradish with the mayonnaise, if you like. I don't because I enjoy the random bursts of breathtaking hot that you get when you just spread the horseradish around by itself. (If you really like the stuff, you might enjoy preparing it fresh yourself, for which there is a recipe in the box on this page.) I use both the sliced radishes and the butter lettuce as garnish, but that might be overdoing it. One or the other would probably suffice.

The bread, or covering, should not be strong in flavor like the herb bread, nor should it be too light a bread either. Something like the oat-sesame might be just right.

Preparing Horseradish

Fresh horseradish tastes so much better than the commercially prepared stuff, it is worth the short period of suffering required to prepare it yourself. First you will have to grow some or find a place to buy it fresh. Horseradish does best in cool regions, planted in rich, moist soils.

The procedure for its preparation is simple but the fumes involved are overpowering to say the least. All you have to do is peel the root and either grind or grate it. Choose whichever method you are best equipped to use and you feel will be the least painful. I suggest using a meat grinder with fine cutter plates. You need to chop up the root before grinding it. When horseradish is shredded, it is very dry and will require a little vinegar or lemon juice to moisten it. Store in a tightly sealed container in the refrigerator.

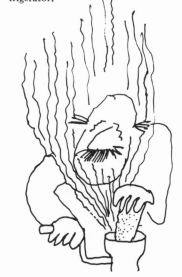

37

Here are three leftover-pork-anything sandwiches.

PORK & SAUERKRAUT

Cooked pork
Sauerkraut
Apple, sliced
Caraway seeds
Mayonnaise
Mustard
Rye bread

Whatever pork you have left over will do, whether it be chops or a roast. You might even have the sauerkraut as well since it is often eaten with pork. If not, just open a small can of it. If you are going to eat the sandwich right away, gently heat the sauerkraut in a saucepan so it steams a little. You could put the pork on top to heat it also.

Cut some thin slices of apple and soak them for a minute in a little lemon juice. Each sandwich should have at least 1/4 apple in it. A nice firm green apple like a Pippin is best.

Spread one piece of the bread with mustard, the other with mayonnaise, and put the meat on the slice with the mustard. Heap lots of sauerkraut on top of the meat and sprinkle lightly with caraway seeds. Lay the slices of apple on top of that and cover with the other slice of bread.

Leftover-pork-anything sandwich number 2.

PORK WITH ORANGE MARMALADE

Cooked pork, sliced
Orange marmalade
Red onion, sliced
Mayonnaise
Red lettuce
Oat-sesame bread

The marmalade must be tart, as it is meant to be, rather than excessively sweet. Use it with discretion. Good luck.

Obviously, porky meat is good with sweet, fruity things. All of these pork sandwiches could be ham sandwiches instead. So if you seldom have leftover pork, buy some slices of ham and try these sandwiches anyway.

Leftover-pork-anything sandwich number 3.

CURRY-FLAVORED PORK SANDWICH

Cooked pork, sliced
Lime juice
Salt
Curried mayonnaise (see box)
Stewed prunes
Red lettuce
Oat-sesame bread

Lay the slices of meat on one piece of bread and squeeze lime juice over the top. Season with salt. Drain the prunes and lay some on top of the meat. Garnish with red lettuce and cover with the other slice of bread, spread generously with curried mayonnaise.

Curried Mayonnaise

1 cup mayonnaise
1/2 teaspoon freshly grated ginger root
1 teaspoon curry powder

To the mayonnaise add the ginger, finely grated, and the curry powder. Mix thoroughly.

In order for these 2 seasonings to work their magic, the mixture must be kept in the refrigerator for at least 20 or 30 minutes before using. If you take a little taste before it is put away and another when it is removed, you will see what I mean.

If you insist on mixing only enough for a single sandwich, 2 tablespoons of mayonnaise will do. As for the curry and ginger, all I can suggest is a pinch of each. In this case I would use dry, ground ginger rather than bother with fresh.

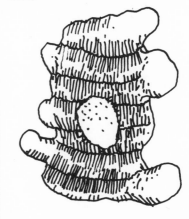

Cooking Pork Sausage Patties

Make the patties thin and a little larger than sandwich size. They will shrink somewhat, but if the meat is lean, not much. Start with the patties in a covered cold frying pan over medium-low heat. If the meat is very lean, you might actually have to oil the pan, but don't get carried away. About 10 minutes after the meat begins to sizzle, turn the patties and take the cover off. You should be able to tell by looking at the first side, now up, how long the second side needs to cook. Remember that the second side has already steamed under the cover, so it will take less time.

You can really eat this sandwich anytime: breakfast, lunch, or dinner.

COUNTRY SAUSAGE BREAKFAST SANDWICH

1/4 pound homemade country
    sausage patty or 4 sausage links
Mustard
Mayonnaise
Spinach
Raisin bread

This sandwich is best eaten hot, with the raisin bread toasted. The mustard, Dijon-style of course, tastes particularly good spread on hot pork sausage, and the aroma will knock you out, figuratively speaking. The fact that the sandwich is warm does not seem to bother the spinach one whit, but if you prefer, try using alfalfa sprouts as a garnish.

Most butchers grind their own sausage meat, but I think it is often too fatty or worse. I prefer to grind my own, using an inexpensive cut such as a portion of the shoulder butt. Buy whatever is cheap at the time, keeping in mind that the whole point is to make lean sausage and paying 49 cents a pound for a lump of fat and bone isn't going to get you there. To make 4 servings of good country sausage use:

1 pound lean pork, freshly ground
1 teaspoon sage
1/2 teaspoon crushed chile pequins
1/4 teaspoon coarse ground black pepper
1/4 teaspoon freshly grated nutmeg

Trim off most of the fat, but don't bother trying to get it all. Grind the meat in your kitchen grinder, and with a large cooking fork, mix all the seasonings into the meat. Mix thoroughly but don't make a paste out of it. Refrigerate overnight before using to give the flavors time to blend.

This one should come as no surprise after Pork with Orange Marmalade.

MARINATED LAMB WITH MINT JELLY & ALMONDS

2 tablespoons olive oil
1 clove garlic
Cooked lamb, sliced
2 teaspoons lemon juice
Mayonnaise
Almonds, slivered
Spinach
Mint jelly

Smash the garlic clove * and saute in the oil for 1 or 2 minutes over medium-low heat. Add the slices of lamb and the lemon juice and continue cooking for another 2 minutes. Allow the meat to cool before using. Lay it on a slice of bread, spread with mayonnaise, and sprinkle with almond slivers. Garnish with spinach and cover with another slice of bread spread with mint jelly.

* Lay a clove of garlic on a cutting board and with one hand hold the flat side of a big, broad knife, like a French kitchen knife, on top of the clove. With the other hand, strike the side of the knife right over the garlic clove a smart blow and you will smash the clove flat.

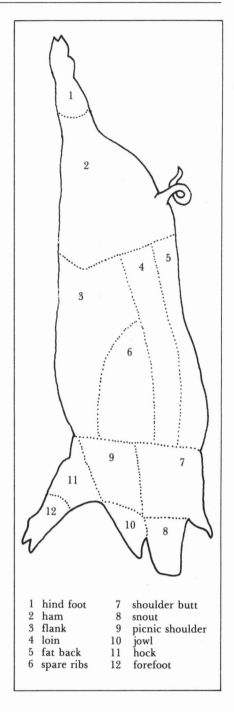

1	hind foot	7	shoulder butt
2	ham	8	snout
3	flank	9	picnic shoulder
4	loin	10	jowl
5	fat back	11	hock
6	spare ribs	12	forefoot

This steak tartare sort of thing gets cooked a little and turns out like a meat loaf that didn't get cooked very much.

GROUND BEEF
FOR COLD SANDWICHES

(4 servings)

1 egg, beaten
1 1/2 teaspoons red, Louisiana
    hot sauce (not Tabasco)
1 teaspoon Lea & Perrins
    Worcestershire sauce
1 clove garlic, pressed
1 1/2 teaspoons whole oregano
1 teaspoon salt
1/2 teaspoon coarse ground
    black pepper
1 pound very lean and freshly
    ground beef
3 large green onions, chopped
1 cup croutons

To the beaten egg, add the seasonings and mix well. When pressing the garlic, be sure to add the pulp that is squeezed through along with the juice. As you add the oregano, crush the leaves a bit with your fingers.

Put the ground beef into a 2-quart mixing bowl and spread it out a bit over the bottom. Sprinkle both the onions and croutons on the meat and pour the egg-seasoning mixture over that. With a cooking fork stir everything together as thoroughly as possible without making mush out of it. Then shape it into a patty about 1 1/2 inches thick.

Sprinkle a light layer of salt over the bottom of a frying pan and heat until it begins to smoke. Put in the meat and cook at a high temperature for 3 or 4 minutes on each side. It should be seared on the outside and very rare inside.

The meat is meant to be eaten cold, but it might be difficult to wait. It should be kept in the refrigerator and sliced up as you need it. There is enough to make 3 huge sandwiches or 4 large ones.

If there is a bit of pot roast hiding in the corner of your refrigerator, put it to good use in your next sandwich.

MOCK BEEF STROGANOFF

Cooked beef, thinly sliced
Sour Cream
Marinated mushrooms (see recipe
  page 92)
Red onion, sliced
Salt
Pepper
Oat-sesame bread

Lay the meat on one slice of bread and season it with salt and pepper if necessary. On top of that lay the onion and spread liberally with sour cream. Drain the mushrooms, either homemade or store bought, and put them on top of the sour cream. Cover with a slice of bread.

Another leftover sandwich: The very thought of this one will give some people cold chills, but genuine liver lovers will love it.

COLD LIVER SANDWICH

Cooked calf liver, thinly sliced
Red onion, thinly sliced
Dill pickle, thinly sliced
Mayonnaise
Spinach
Oat-sesame bread

After all that thin slicing, the procedure gets real simple. Stack everything up and eat it.

The Slippery Sandwich Remedy

How do you keep the inside of a sandwich inside? How do you keep it from squirting out all over your lap?

This is most apt to happen when you use a French roll because the roll, being thick and crusty, requires a good strong bite and therefore a firm grip. In the process of biting and gripping, the insides are simply squeezed out.

The remedy is to avoid lubricating both sides of the covering, whatever it is, with mayonnaise and mustard. Spread only one side, a slice of bread or half a roll, with mayonnaise and lay the filling on the other side, the *bare* slice of bread or roll. The idea is that the filling is not apt to slide around on the dry bread. Spread the mustard directly on the filling, stacking the garnish on top and covering with the piece of bread or roll with mayonnaise on it.

A salad filling is a real problem. The only remedy is not to use a hard roll in the first place. For more information regarding salad fillings and their problems, see the box on page 54.

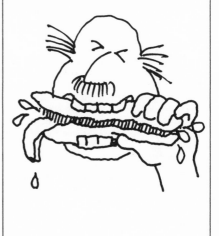

Making Mayonnaise

(about 1 1/4 cups)

2 egg yolks
1/2 teaspoon salt
1/2 teaspoon dry mustard
1 cup olive oil
2 tablespoons lemon juice or white
    wine vinegar

Making mayonnaise is not so difficult as it is time consuming and tricky in the sense that sometimes it works and sometimes it doesn't. You need to be relaxed and in a positive frame of mind to undertake the making of mayonnaise. You will also need someone to help you.

Make sure all the ingredients, as well as the mixing bowl, are at room temperature. Beat the egg yolks and add the salt and dry mustard. While one person is beating the mixture with an egg beater, the other will add the oil, 1/2 teaspoon at a time. Do not stop beating the mixture and keep adding the oil, slowly dribbling it out of the 1/2 teaspoon. When the oil is used up, the mixture should be thick and emulsified.

If you are able to do this without mishap, you should consider yourself lucky. Generally what happens is the mixture will separate or break up as you are beating it because you have added the oil too quickly. It is unlikely to happen after the first 1/2 cup of oil has been added, but whenever it happens, put aside what you have been working on and start over with a new egg yolk, this time, *sans* seasoning, and add the balance of the oil very slowly and carefully while beating with the egg beater. When this has combined, blend in the separated mixture with the new, just as if it were oil, slowly and carefully.

The last thing to do is stir in the lemon juice. You will be thinning the mayonnaise as well as flavoring it. I feel that 2 tablespoons is a maximum, but you might feel differently. You might also want to add a bit more salt.

There are two sandwich-meat sausages I cannot refuse, and this is one of them.

LIVERWURST SANDWICH

Liverwurst
Dill pickle, sliced
Mustard
Mayonnaise
Lettuce
Rye bread

On one slice of bread spread the liverwurst and on the other the mayonnaise. Spread the mustard on the meat, put the pickles on top and then add the lettuce. Cover with the other slice of bread.

The second sausage to which I am addicted is dry Italian salami. I have the butcher slice it very thin for me from one of those big, long sausages. Basically the sandwich is the same as above except I would be inclined to leave out the pickle and would use a french roll rather than the rye bread. Eat this sandwich along with a fistful of pepperoncini.

Try this sandwich when you bake egg bread.

"SWISS" CHEESE ON EGG BREAD

Emmenthal cheese
Mayonnaise
Egg bread

There are two important conditions which must be met if this extraordinarily simple sandwich is to match its potential. The bread must be fresh, preferably still warm, and the cheese must be of a good quality. It should be firm but not rubbery, delicately sweet and nutty, rather than bitter. There are probably far more bad "Swiss" cheeses than there are good ones, and the only way to find out which is which, is to taste them. This of course precludes buying prepackaged cheese, so find a good cheese shop and taste before you buy. Keep in mind that just because it's imported, doesn't mean it's good, and just because it's domestic, does not mean it's bad.

While the bread is still warm, cut a couple of thick slices and spread one with mayonnaise. Cut a single, thick slice of good Swiss Emmenthal cheese at room temperature and sandwich between the slices of bread. I intend to institute this sandwich, as many of them as I can consume, as an egg-bread-baking tradition.

A traditional sandwich.

GRILLED CHEESE

Sharp Cheddar cheese, sliced
Garlic powder
Paprika
Salt
Butter
Rye bread

As far as I am concerned, the whole idea behind a grilled cheese sandwich is to see how much cheese you can pile between two slices of bread. There are limits of course. You don't want all that cheese to end up stuck to the frying pan. Neither should there be so much that some doesn't melt.

Any good quality sharp Cheddar will do. Buy it at a cheese shop or from a butcher, so you will be able to taste it before you buy. It should be a little crumbly but not dry, and certainly sharp but never bitter.

After you pile as much cheese as you dare on one of the slices of bread, season it. A little garlic powder will go a long way, but feel free to use lots of paprika. After seasoning, cover with a second slice of bread. Melt a little butter in a frying pan at low heat. Put in the sandwich and cover it with a saucepan lid. The lid should cover the sandwich but not the frying pan — you don't want to steam the sandwich, just hold in the heat to melt the cheese a little quicker. After 5 minutes or so, turn the sandwich, adding a bit more butter at the same time, and replace the lid. When you hear cheese sizzling in the pan, the sandwich is ready to eat.

I have to have green onions with my grilled cheese sandwiches. Three nice crisp, fresh ones with a little pile of salt to dip them in will generally get me through one sandwich. Although I am not overly fond of sweet pickles, I understand they are also a good accompaniment.

A simple spread and an equally simple sandwich in which to use it.

CREAMED CREAM CHEESE?

8-ounce package cream cheese
1/4 cup chopped green onions
1/4 cup buttermilk
1/4 teaspoon salt

The only trick to this spread is getting the right buttermilk. The kind I use is made by Tuttle and is a Bulgarian style, cultured buttermilk. I cannot imagine there being a better one, so unless you can buy Tuttle's, you might try substituting sour cream. In any case, just combine the above ingredients, and you will have a spread I consider far superior to straight cream cheese. Here is one possibility for a creamed cream cheese sandwich.

Cream cheese spread (above)
Cucumber, sliced
Mayonnaise
Egg bread

Additional suggestions for sandwiches and garnishes on page 87. Simple enough, you're on your own.

The cheese from the bread makes a very good spread.

POTTED CHEDDAR CHEESE

(about 3 cups)

1 pound sharp Cheddar cheese
1 teaspoon Italian herbs (see
   page 30)
1/4 teaspoon dill weed
1/2 teaspoon dill seed
1/2 teaspoon garlic powder
1/2 teaspoon coarse ground
   black pepper
1/2 teaspoon salt
1 cup buttermilk

As you may have noticed, this is the same recipe as the cheese for the cheese bread with the addition of buttermilk. As in the preceding recipe for creamed cheese, I use Tuttle's Bulgarian style, cultured buttermilk.

Grate the cheese while it is still cold and mix in the seasonings immediately. Be sure to sprinkle the herbs all over the top of the cheese as you mix, so they don't all end up in one or two lumps. Let both the cheese and buttermilk warm up to room temperature, then mix thoroughly. Pack in a container with a good tight lid and store in the refrigerator overnight before using.

This is a nice spread to keep on hand for snacks. It is very good all by itself spread on crackers, whole wheat preferably, and it is best of all on celery. Just lay a long pile of it right down the trough of a crisp celery stalk and eat that along with a handful of whole wheat crackers like Wheat Thins. Oh, and don't forget the cold bottle of beer. Of course this spread is also good in sandwiches.

Cheddar cheese spread
Tomato, sliced
Mustard
Mayonnaise
Alfalfa sprouts
Oat-sesame bread

Spread lots of the cheese on one slice of bread and mayonnaise on the other. Spread just a little mustard on the cheese and cover with tomato slices, sprouts, and the other slice of bread.

This sandwich should bring joy to the hearts of the blue-veined cheese lovers.

ROQUEFORT WITH APPLE

1/4 cup crumbled Roquefort
    cheese
2 tablespoons chopped celery
2 tablespoons mayonnaise
1/4 apple, sliced
Egg bread

Crumble up the Roquefort as best you can. It is easiest when the cheese is cold. You may use any blue-veined cheese, but Roquefort is the best. The celery will be a little difficult to measure, so don't worry about it. Lightly stir the cheese, celery, and mayonnaise together. Don't try to homogenize it. Spread the mixture on a slice of bread and put the apple slices on top. Cover with another slice of bread.

A basic turkey sandwich, but a weird choice of bread.

TURKEY ON RAISIN BREAD

Turkey, sliced
Mustard
Paprika
Salt
Coarse ground black pepper
Lettuce
Mayonnaise
Raisin bread

Lay the turkey on one slice of bread and spread it lightly with mustard. Sprinkle with lots of paprika and a little salt and pepper. Cover with lettuce and a second slice of bread, spread with a generous amount of mayonnaise.

A little pretentious for a sandwich you say. Why not, I say.

FLAMBEED CHICKEN LIVER SANDWICH

(2 servings)

3/4 pound chicken livers
3 tablespoons butter
2 tablespoons brandy
1 tablespoon flour
3/4 cup chicken broth
Salt
Coarse ground black pepper
1 tablespoon lemon juice
2 green onions
2 French rolls

Melt the butter in a 6-inch frying pan over medium-low heat and saute the livers for 3 or 4 minutes. Pour the brandy over them and light it immediately, stirring things a bit until the flame goes out. Sprinkle the flour on the livers and continue stirring for a moment, then add the broth. Simmer over a low heat until the liquid has partially evaporated and thickened, which should take about 10 minutes. Turn off the heat, season with salt and pepper, add the lemon juice, and stir a little.

Cut the rolls in half and scoop out some of the dough from each side to make a hollow. Butter each side lightly and place under the broiler for that moment, buttered side up, to heat. It is a proved fact that if you ever take your eyes off bread under a broiler, it will burn instantly. Fill one-half of each roll with the livers and sprinkle the top liberally with a chopped green onion. Cover with the other half of the roll and eat while warm.

Use a well-seasoned 6-inch cast-iron frying pan or a heavy steel omelet pan for frying eggs. Preheat the pan at medium-low heat with a little butter in it and start the egg before the butter turns brown. Break the yolk immediately. As soon as the egg becomes firm enough to turn, turn it. Do not let it get crisp around the edge. After you turn the egg, shut off the heat and season. Leave the egg in the pan until you are ready to put it in the sandwich.

A good sandwich when all you have are eggs and very little time.

FRIED EGG WITH CURRY

1 egg, fried (see box this page)
Onion, sliced
Curried mayonnaise (see recipe
        page 39)
Spinach
Raisin bread

Fry the egg "over easy" and be sure to break the yoke. Lay it on a bare slice of bread and put the slices of onion on top. I hope it will be a nice sweet onion like a red Italian or a mild Bermuda onion. Add a few leaves of fresh spinach. Cover with another slice of bread spread with the curried mayonnaise. If you do not happen to have any, sprinkle a pinch of curry powder on the egg and use plain mayonnaise.

Good hot or cold.

ANOTHER FRIED EGG SANDWICH

1 egg, fried
Mayonnaise
Mustard
Dill pickle, sliced
Alfalfa sprouts
Herb bread

If a fried egg sandwich is to be eaten hot, you might want to toast the bread. Don't bother if it is to be eaten cold.

Have you any henny friends who will lay you some eggs?

EGG SALAD SANDWICH
(2 servings)

2 hard-boiled eggs, chopped
1/4 teaspoon dill seed
1/2 teaspoon dry mustard
1/4 teaspoon coarse ground
        black pepper
1/4 teaspoon salt
2 teaspoons lemon juice
1/3 cup mayonnaise
2 green onions, chopped
Alfalfa sprouts
Herb bread

Try to mix the salad 15 or 20 minutes ahead of time to give the flavors a chance to blend and strengthen. Use lots of sprouts as garnish to hold everything together.

Additional suggestions for sandwiches and garnishes on page 92.

Egg Slicer

If you slice no more than 3 hard-boiled eggs all the rest of your life, this gadget is worth the little it costs.

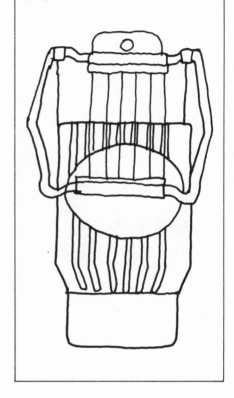

A Salad Sandwich Trick

Salad sandwiches oftentimes have an oozy quality about them. At best they are an inconvenience to eat. The right garnish — alfalfa sprouts — will help to alleviate the problem.

Much like the wire over which stucco is applied, the sprouts provide a base for the salad filling and hold it all together.

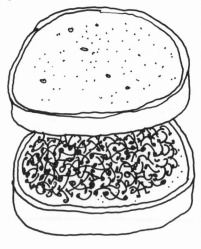

A waste of time, if you don't like chicken.

CHICKEN SANDWICH

Chicken, sliced
Paprika
Salt
Coarse ground black pepper
Mayonnaise
Mustard
Alfalfa sprouts
Herb bread

Don't skimp on the paprika, mayonnaise, or alfalfa sprouts — or anything else for that matter.

Introducing pita or Arabic bread, in which, obviously, you can put anything.

LEFTOVER TUNA & NOODLES IN PITA

Cooked tuna and noodle casserole
Butter
Salt
Cayenne
Tomato, sliced
Pita (see recipe in box)

Melt some butter in a small frying pan over medium-low heat. Scoop up some of the casserole and place in the pan when heated. Flatten with a spatula to make a patty about 1/2 inch thick and a little smaller around than the pita. Saute until crisp, then turn. Add more butter if necessary and salt to taste, sprinkling the top with a pinch of cayenne as well.

The pita should be heating in the oven meanwhile, but be careful it does not become crisp. When all is ready, cut the flat loaves in half and fill with the patty and tomato slices. Serve warm.

Pita, or Arabic Bread
(makes 6 flat loaves)

1 1/4 cups warm water
1 tablespoon yeast
1/4 teaspoon sugar
2 cups unbleached white flour
2 teaspoons salt
2 tablespoons olive oil
2 cups whole wheat flour
Cornmeal

If you have not read chapter 2, Making Bread, you should do so before attempting this recipe. In a bowl, thoroughly dissolve the yeast and sugar in the warm water, then add the white flour. Stir until smooth and set in a warm place for about 20 minutes. Fold in remaining ingredients and knead thoroughly. When you have finished kneading, return dough to cleaned and oiled bowl, cover with a damp cloth, and again set in a warm place to rise, this time for 40 or 50 minutes or until its size has about doubled.

After the dough has risen, punch it down, divide it into 6 equal portions, and roll each portion into a ball. Roll each of the portions out flat with a rolling pin until they are about 1/8 inch thick and no less than 6 inches across. Be sure there are no folds or seams in the dough. Set aside to rise for 20 or 30 minutes.

Preheat the oven to 500 degrees. Dust a cookie sheet with cornmeal, arrange 2 or 3 of the flat loaves on top and dust those with just a bit more cornmeal. Put the cookie sheet directly on the bottom of the oven and bake for 5 minutes. Then move the sheet up to the lowest rack and bake for an additional 5 minutes or until the loaves are puffed and browned. Repeat the process for the rest of the loaves. Cool on a rack, then wrap in foil to keep them soft. When cut in half, the loaves form a pocket in which to put the casserole filling.

Pita can be used with all kinds of casserole fillings including such diversities as ratatouille (see recipe page 67) or eggplant, tomato, and chickpea casserole (see page 109).

My friend and butcher, Bob Young, wouldn't be caught dead eating one of these sandwiches, but maybe he just looks Chinese.

CHINATOWN TUNA SALAD SANDWICH
(4 servings)

12 1/2-ounce can light chunk tuna
1 cup mayonnaise
2 teaspoons dry mustard
1/2 teaspoon grated, fresh ginger
   root
2 teaspoons soy sauce
1 tablespoon lemon juice
1 teaspoon chopped, fresh cilantro
1/2 cup green onions, chopped
Alfalfa sprouts
Oat-sesame bread

While the can of tuna is draining, mix the balance of the salad ingredients. When the tuna is completely drained, add it to the other ingredients, except alfalfa sprouts and bread, and mix. Spread liberally on a slice of bread and cover with sprouts. Close the sandwich with a second slice of bread. By the way, cilantro is also called Chinese parsley.

A rich little poor boy sandwich.

OYSTER LOAF
(2 or 3 servings)

1 dozen medium-sized oysters
2 cups bread crumbs
1/2 cube butter
1 long loaf French bread
1/2 cup tartar sauce (see box
   this page)
1 1/2 cups shredded iceberg lettuce
1/2 lemon
1 large tomato, sliced
Salt

Melt butter in large frying pan over medium-low heat. Drain and dry oysters, roll in bread crumbs until covered, and saute in butter. Cook for about 5 minutes, turning gently with a fork.

Cut the loaf of bread in half lengthwise, hollow out each half, and spread with butter. If there is any butter left in the pan after frying the oysters, use that, spreading it with a pastry brush. Heat the bread in the oven or under the broiler for just a moment. Spread both halves with tartar sauce and lay shredded lettuce all along the bottom half. Lay the oysters on top of the lettuce and squeeze lemon juice over them. Arrange sliced tomato on top and salt. Cover with the other half loaf and divide into 2 or 3 portions. Serve warm.

Try this same sandwich using breaded scallops instead of oysters. Unfortunately, this variation is beyond the means of all the poor boys I know.

Tartar Sauce
(about 1 1/2 cups)

1 cup mayonnaise
1 teaspoon Dijon-style mustard
1 pinch cayenne
1/2 teaspoon salt
1 teaspoon lemon juice
1/4 cup chopped green onions
1 tablespoon chopped fresh cilantro
1 tablespoon chopped fresh parsley
2 tablespoons chopped dill pickle

This sauce will taste best after the flavors have had time to blend. For that reason you should try to mix it up well before you plan to use it.

A little eastern herbal magic worked on a few dead shrimp, makes an elegant salad sandwich mixture.

CURRIED SHRIMP SALAD WITH APPLE
(2 servings)

4 tablespoons curried mayon-
   naise (see recipe page 39)
1 large green onion or scallion
1/4 pound small cooked shrimp
Salt
Pepper
4 slices rye bread
Butter
Shredded coconut
1/2 cored apple
Lemon
Butter lettuce

Put the mayonnaise in a bowl and add the onion, chopped, using as much of the green part as possible. Add the shrimp and season to taste with salt and pepper.

Lightly butter 4 slices of bread, spread the salad mixture on 2 of them and sprinkle with a little coconut. Cut the apple into very thin slices and lay on top, then squeeze lemon juice over them. Include the lettuce and cover with the buttered bread.

Using either fresh or leftover fish, this sandwich is good eaten hot or cold.

FISH SANDWICH

Filet of sole
Butter
Lemon juice
Salt
Coarse ground black pepper
Thyme
Mayonnaise
Green onion, finely chopped
Alfalfa sprouts
Herb bread

Saute the fish in butter and lemon juice and season with salt, pepper, and a pinch of thyme. If the fish is left over, just squeeze a little lemon juice over it and season if necessary. Any fish will do, providing the bones have been removed.

Mix the mayonnaise with the chopped green onion and spread on a slice of bread. The fish goes on the other slice with the sprouts on top.

This sandwich is a little rough on those in whose direction you happen to breathe, but it tastes good.

SARDINE WITH ONION

Sardines
Lemon juice
Salt
Red onion
Mayonnaise
Mustard
Lettuce
Oat-sesame bread

Lay the sardines, head to tail, on a slice of bread spread with mustard and squeeze a little lemon juice over them. Salt to taste and cover with thin slices of red onion. Add the lettuce and cover with another slice of bread that has been spread with mayonnaise.

This is a good way to use one of those unfortunate avocados offered at a bargain price, because it has been squeezed to death.

AVOCADO SANDWICH

1/2 avocado
1/2 teaspoon lemon juice
1 green onion, chopped
Salt
Coarse ground black pepper
Mayonnaise
Alfalfa sprouts
Herb bread

Mash the avocado together with the lemon juice. Season with salt and pepper and mix with the chopped onion. Spread on a slice of bread and cover with sprouts. Close with second slice of bread spread liberally with mayonnaise.

About Avocados

On the West Coast, avocados are available all year long but are best during the summer months. The "Haas," a Guatemalan type is generally available from April to October. This avocado has a rather thick, rough skin, a wonderful flavor, and firm but easily spread meat. It will ripen beautifully but must be handled carefully because it will bruise if you look at it. The rest of the year we have to settle for a hybrid avocado called "Fuerte." It has a smooth, thin skin and rubbery, tasteless meat. It never seems to really ripen and, as far as I am concerned, is not worth buying.

The easiest way to get at the meat is to cut the fruit in half, around the pit, and open it by twisting the two halves apart. Lever out the pit with the knife, cut the avocado into slices, and then peel off the skin. If you only intend to use half, use the one without the pit and leave it in the other half. Store it in the refrigerator in an airtight container. For some reason or other, the pit seems to keep the meat from turning black. Unless you are going to use the avocado slices immediately, they should have some lime or lemon juice squeezed over them. This will also prevent the meat from turning black — in addition, lime or lemon juice tastes terrific with avocado.

For a real taste treat simply open up a perfectly ripened "Haas," pop out the pit, squeeze a little lime juice on each half, salt lightly, and eat with a spoon.

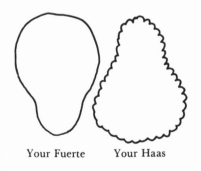

Your Fuerte   Your Haas

My mother made this sandwich for me thirty years ago.

CHOPPED OLIVE

(2 servings)

4 1/2-ounce can chopped olives
2 teaspoons olive oil
1 teaspoon lemon juice
Garlic
1 pinch thyme
1 pinch salt
1 pinch pepper
Mayonnaise
Alfalfa sprouts
Herb bread

Drain the olives and put in a bowl with the balance of the ingredients. Squeeze the garlic through a press. Mix the ingredients, except mayonnaise, alfalfa sprouts, and bread, thoroughly. Spread one slice of bread with mayonnaise and put the chopped olive mixture on top. Cover with sprouts and another slice of bread.

This sandwich should not be allowed to sit around very long, because it is very runny and the olive mixture will soak the bread.

Mother sez: "Eat those crusts!"

Combination Sandwiches
(In Which There Are Two or More Ingredients)

Add an egg to a BLT and the resulting BELT will help get you started in the morning.

BACON, EGG, LETTUCE & TOMATO

3 strips bacon
1 egg, fried (see box page 52)
Salt
Pepper
Rye bread
Butter
1/2 tomato, sliced
Iceberg lettuce
Mayonnaise

Fry the bacon first and when it has become very crisp, set it aside on a paper towel to drain. While the egg is frying, toast the bread and butter it. Season the egg with salt and pepper and lay it on one of the pieces of buttered toast. Put the bacon on top, then the tomato slices and lettuce. Cover with the second piece of toast, spread liberally with mayonnaise. A friend of mine once told me that except for obvious physical limitations, it is impossible to put too much mayonnaise on a BLT. I assume that this fact must also be true of a BELT.

Marinated Olive Salad

6-ounce can pitted green olives, drained
6-ounce can pitted black olives, drained
1/3 cup Italian pepperoncini, quartered
    lengthwise
1 large sweet red onion, thinly sliced
    and separated into rings
1/2 cup chopped celery
1/4 cup olive oil
1/4 cup wine vinegar
1 teaspoon oregano
Salt
Pepper

Put all of the ingredients into a bowl and toss, so the oil and vinegar cover everything. Serve as an antipasto or salad. Store in the refrigerator.

Almost a traditional cheeseburger.

BACON & CHEESE BURGER

Lean ground beef
Cheddar cheese
Bacon
Onion, sliced
Tomato, sliced
Lettuce, your choice
Mayonnaise
Mustard
French roll, whole wheat
    English muffin, or hamburger
    bun

Using a good lean ground beef, make a fairly thin patty, the shape of the French roll or whatever you are using for a covering. Start with a hot pan and fry the meat for a short while, but don't cook the meat until it is all dry and shriveled. Put a thin layer of cheese on top as soon as it has been turned.

Cook the bacon in another pan until it is crisp and set it aside on a paper towel to drain. Add a little butter to the same pan and saute some slices of yellow or white onion until they are soft and beginning to turn brown. When everything is cooked, assemble the ingredients in your covering. Be prepared to eat a potentially messy but delicious sandwich. You might want to turn to page 43 to find out how to keep the mess to a minimum.

An abbreviated version of the wonderful French vegetable casserole makes a wonderful sandwich ingredient.

HASTY TASTY RATATOUILLE

1/4-1/2 cup olive oil
1 eggplant
2 medium-sized onions, chopped
1 large clove garlic
2 cups tomatoes, peeled and
   chopped or 1 pint homemade
   tomato sauce or two 8-ounce
   cans tomato sauce, plain or
   seasoned
Parsley
Salt
Pepper

While 1/4 cup of olive oil is heating in a Dutch oven
or any other tall-sided pan which will contain spattering
oil, cut the unpeeled eggplant into cubes about 1/2 inch
square. Saute the eggplant, onion, and garlic in the oil,
stirring constantly until evenly but lightly browned. Add
more oil as necessary. Add the tomatoes and simmer
gently until thickened and the vegetables are soft and
tender. Season with salt, pepper, and chopped fresh
parsley.

Sometime try a recipe for the complete version of
ratatouille.

Presenting three great sandwiches featuring the one and only H. T. Ratatouille.

H. T. RATATOUILLE & CHEESE

H. T. Ratatouille
Cheese, sliced
Alfalfa sprouts
Oat-sesame bread

All three of these sandwiches are meant to be eaten cold. Of course the ratatouille may be heated, but it might become too runny to use in a sandwich. It is delicious at room temperature and I prefer to eat it that way — in a sandwich or otherwise. The alfalfa sprouts are excellent with ratatouille and also help to hold it all together and keep it inside the sandwich (see box page 54). A relish is not really necessary, but either mayonnaise or sour cream could be used in moderation.

I suggest using a sharp Cheddar or Kasseri cheese in this first sandwich. A good Emmenthal would work also providing its flavor was not completely lost in the ratatouille. Cover one slice of bread with cheese and spread a thick layer of ratatouille on top. Cover with lots of sprouts and another slice of bread.

H. T. RATATOUILLE & CHICKEN

H. T. Ratatouille
Chicken, sliced
Alfalfa sprouts
Oat-sesame bread

Assemble this sandwich the same as the first one, starting with the chicken. Don't be afraid to season these sandwiches with a little salt and pepper if necessary; paprika would also be good on all three sandwiches.

H. T. RATATOUILLE & EGG

H. T. Ratatouille
1 egg, fried or scrambled
Alfalfa sprouts or spinach
Oat-sesame bread

You have a choice in the preparation of this sandwich. You may fry the egg and assemble the sandwich as above, or you may scramble the egg with the ratatouille. In the latter case, the egg and ratatouille should be mixed together and poured into a preheated and buttered pan. Cook as you would a patty, trying to keep it all in one piece. Don't overcook! This sandwich might require a little mayonnaise. Use spinach as a garnish.

An excellent covering to use with ratatouille is pita, an Arabic bread. There is a recipe on page 55.

A "Goodyear" avocado will not do here.

AVOCADO & BACON

Avocado, mashed
Bacon, fried
Lemon juice
Sour cream or mayonnaise
Spinach
Herb bread

Fry the bacon crisp and drain it on a paper towel. Spread the mashed avocado on a slice of bread and crumble the bacon over it. Squeeze a little lemon juice on top and cover with spinach. Cover with another slice of bread spread with sour cream or mayonnaise.

Another sandwich requiring a good and ripe avocado.

HAM & AVOCADO

Ham, sliced
Avocado
Green onion, chopped
Mustard
Mayonnaise
Red lettuce
Herb bread

Mash the avocado and mix with the chopped onion. Spread on a slice of bread and cover with mayonnaise. Spread another slice of bread lightly with mustard and put the ham on that and the lettuce on top. Cover with the first slice of bread.

This method of preparation is second only to grinding as a means of dealing with an unattractive piece of leftover meat.

BEEF OR HAM & CHEESE JULIENNE

Beef or ham
Swiss cheese
Mayonnaise
Horseradish
Chives, chopped
Summer savory
Salt
Coarse ground black pepper
Lettuce or alfalfa sprouts
Rye bread

Cut the meat and cheese into matchstick-sized pieces and moisten with enough mayonnaise to make the mixture spreadable. About 2 tablespoons is sufficient for one sandwich. Season with horseradish, chives, savory, salt, and pepper, and garnish with either lettuce or sprouts. If the filling looks as though it's going to exit the sandwich onto your lap, you had better use sprouts. Try rye bread as a covering.

Leftover Vegetables in Vinaigrette Sauce

This is a good way to use the vegetables that were left over along with the meat you are preparing a sandwich of. It is also a good thing to eat along with that sandwich.

Vinaigrette sauce, like marinade, is simply olive oil and vinegar with a few additional ingredients. It is in fact a salad dressing. A little garlic could be included with a pinch of dry mustard and an herb.

The vegetables can be anything, including boiled potatoes, peas, corn, and so on. Since these will be cooked, it is nice to add something fresh like sliced tomatoes and green onions.

Using leftover vegetables this way is far better than reheating them, unless of course they are already in a sauce or gravy.

An oldie but goodie.

CLUB SANDWICH

Cooked chicken, sliced
Salt
Paprika
Tomato, sliced
Mayonnaise
Bacon
Butter lettuce
Egg bread, toasted

Lay the slices of chicken on a piece of toasted bread and season lightly with salt and paprika. On top, put the tomato slices, spread mayonnaise on them, and crumble the bacon over that. Garnish with the lettuce and cover with a second piece of toast.

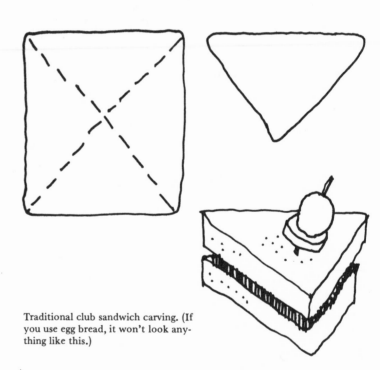

Traditional club sandwich carving. (If you use egg bread, it won't look anything like this.)

Despite the ordinary ingredients, I doubt that many have tried this combination.

BACON & EGG & CHEESE

Bacon
Egg
Paprika
Sharp Cheddar cheese, sliced
Dill pickle, sliced
Alfalfa sprouts
Mayonnaise
Rye bread

Fry the bacon crisp and drain on a paper towel. Fry the egg next and after seasoning with paprika and maybe a little salt and pepper, melt the cheese on top. Put the egg and cheese on a slice of bread and crumble the bacon on top. Garnish with a couple of slices of pickle and the sprouts. Cover with a second slice of bread spread with mayonnaise.

Another breakfast sandwich, good any time of the day.

HAM & EGG & CHEESE

Ham, sliced
Egg, hard-boiled and sliced
Swiss cheese, sliced
Dill pickle, sliced
Mayonnaise
Mustard
Butter lettuce
Rye bread

Assemble in a manner that pleases you. A little salt and pepper might be in order. Don't use too much of any one of the three major ingredients. Use plenty of mayonnaise and lettuce.

An important ingredient in the next sandwich.

MIXED ANTIPASTO
(about 1 1/2 cups)

2 1/4-ounce can sliced
   ripe olives
3 1/2-ounce jar cocktail
   onions, halved
2-ounce can anchovies
1/2 cup Italian pepperoncini,
   halved
1/3 cup olive oil
1/3 cup white wine vinegar
2 teaspoons tomato paste
1 pinch coarse ground black
   pepper
1/4 teaspoon salt
1/4 teaspoon basil

Drain the olives and put them in a mixing bowl. Drain and cut onions in half before adding to bowl. Drain anchovies and add. Pull or cut stems off pepperoncini, slice in half lengthwise, and add. Include balance of ingredients and mix thoroughly but gently. Keep tightly sealed in refrigerator.

This recipe makes enough for approximately 2 or 3 submarine sandwiches.

1 long loaf French bread
Mayonnaise
Iceberg lettuce, shredded
1 cup mixed antipasto
1/4 pound Italian dry salami,
   sliced
1/2 pound Swiss cheese, sliced
Mustard
1/4 pound baked ham, sliced

Cut a loaf of French bread in half lengthwise and remove some of the bread from each half to form a hollow down the center. Spread the bottom half liberally with mayonnaise and lay the shredded lettuce on top. Spoon the antipasto mix on top of the lettuce. Add the salami next, then the cheese. Spread a little mustard on the cheese before adding the layer of ham. Cover with the other half loaf and cut into 2 or 3 portions.

The Scandinavians would make this open-face and so may you, if you wish.

SARDINES & CHEESE

Sardines
Gruyere cheese, thinly sliced
Tomato, sliced
Spinach
Mayonnaise
Oat-sesame bread

Drain the oil from the sardines and lay on a slice of bread, head to tail. On top, lay a few slices of the cheese and tomato. Salt the tomato if necessary. Cover with spinach and another slice of bread spread liberally with mayonnaise.

If you don't want to use this recipe in a sandwich, it is already a salad.

CURRIED CHICKEN & FRUIT SALAD
(8 servings)

1 cup cooked and shredded chicken
1/4 cup slivered almonds
1/4 cup chopped celery
1/2 cup quartered seedless grapes
1 cup diced cantaloupe

1/2 cup mayonnaise
1/4 teaspoon curry powder
1/4 teaspoon ground ginger
2 teaspoons lime juice
1/2 teaspoon salt
1 pinch coarse ground black
   pepper

Alfalfa sprouts
Raisin bread

Prepare the first five ingredients and put them in a mixing bowl. Mix the next group of ingredients thoroughly and add to the first. Stir lightly to combine. Allow 30 minutes before using so the flavors will build up a bit. Butter the slice of bread upon which the salad is to be spread to prevent it from becoming soggy. Be sure to use enough sprouts to help hold the salad in the sandwich.

A combination fruit sandwich that is not sweet.

AVOCADO & CHOPPED OLIVE

(2 servings)

1/2 avocado
Mayonnaise
4 1/2-ounce can chopped ripe
    olives
Salt
Pepper
Alfalfa sprouts
Herb bread

Cut the avocado half into slices and peel. Lay them on two slices of bread and spread by mashing them. Spread with mayonnaise, then cover with the drained chopped olives. Season to taste with salt and pepper and garnish with sprouts. Cover each with another slice of bread.

Tired of peanut butter and jam? Try this instead.

PEANUT BUTTER SPECIAL

Peanut butter
Raisins
Cucumber, sliced
Mayonnaise
Egg bread

Spread one slice of bread with lots of peanut butter and the other with mayonnaise. The raisins and cucumber slices go in between.

Or this.

PEANUT BUTTER EXTRA SPECIAL

Peanut butter
Raisins
Banana, sliced
Butter lettuce
Mayonnaise
Egg bread

Spread one slice of bread with lots of peanut butter and the other with mayonnaise. The raisins, banana slices, and butter lettuce go in between.

Open-Face Sandwiches
(In Which Only One Slice of Bread Is Used)

Before feeding the leftover tongue to your dog, please try this recipe.

GROUND TONGUE WITH CURRY
(4 to 6 servings)

2/3 cup mayonnaise
2 teaspoons vinegar
1 teaspoon curry powder
1/2 teaspoon salt
1 pinch cayenne

1/2 pound tongue, ground
1 hard-boiled egg, chopped
1/2 cup chopped green onion

Mix the first group of ingredients thoroughly and set aside. Grind the tongue and add to the curried mayonnaise. After chopping them up, add the egg and onion and stir everything together. Spread on toast and serve with a dab of apple chutney on top.

Apple Chutney
(about 3 cups)

1 small lemon, seeded and minced (including the rind)
1 medium-sized clove garlic
3 cups firm green apples, cored and sliced but not peeled
1/3 cup fresh ginger root, peeled and minced
1 1/2 cups raisins
1 cup apple cider vinegar
1 cup brown sugar
1 teaspoon salt
1/4 teaspoon cayenne

Place all the prepared ingredients in a large frying pan and simmer. Stir occasionally and cook neither too fast nor too long or the whole mess might caramelize. When the apples are soft and tender, turn off heat and cool. Store in a sealed container in the refrigerator.

Making Mustard

Hot mustard is made by mixing dry mustard (I use Colman's) with cold liquids like water, vinegar, or white wine as in Dijon-style mustard. The basic mixture is 2 parts dry mustard to 1 part liquid. To that you may add seasoning to your taste and if you wish, oil, to make the mixture a little less hot. Try the following recipe first and then change it around as you like. Used sparingly, as I'm sure you will, it makes enough mustard for at least 3 sandwiches.

4 teaspoons dry mustard
2 teaspoons water
1/4 teaspoon brown sugar
1 teaspoon olive oil

Thoroughly mix the dry mustard and sugar with the water and let it sit for 10 or 15 minutes. Stir in the olive oil, and the mixture is ready to use. If it is too hot, stir in more oil. Sometime try substituting vinegar for the water. This mixture will have to sit for a longer period of time because initially the combination will taste quite bitter. Remember, this mustard is supposed to be hot. If you have to mix in great amounts of oil before you can stand to eat it, forget it.

Leftover-pork-anything, sandwich number 4.

PORK WITH SESAME SEEDS

Cooked pork
Lea & Perrins Worcestershire Sauce
Butter
Hot mustard (see box)
Sesame seeds, toasted
Green onions
Mayonnaise
Butter lettuce
Oat-sesame bread

Put 1 part Worcestershire sauce and 3 parts butter in a frying pan over medium heat. Cut the pork into bite-sized pieces and fry until brown and crisp but not dried up. If there are drippings and sauce left in the pan, fry the bread on one side until it is lightly toasted. Spread the bread with mayonnaise on the toasted side if you've fried it, and place a leaf of lettuce on top, then the meat. Spread a little of the hot mustard directly on the meat and sprinkle generously with toasted sesame seeds. Use chopped green onion as a garnish. Leftover pork sandwiches numbers 1, 2, and 3, are on pages 38 and 39.

Another leftover sandwich.

HAM SALAD

Cooked ham, ground or minced
Dill pickle, minced
Celery, chopped
Green onion, chopped
Dry mustard
Salt
Pepper
Mayonnaise
Lettuce
Herb bread
Slice of tomato or hard-boiled egg

Mince, chop, and season salad to taste. Assemble in this order, bottom to top: bread, lettuce leaf, salad with a slice of tomato or hard-boiled egg on top.

Not just another ham sandwich.

HAM & ASPARAGUS

Rye bread
Mustard
Cooked ham, sliced
Mayonnaise
Cooked asparagus
Paprika

Spread a little mustard on the bread and lay the ham on top. Spread some mayonnaise on the ham and garnish with cooked asparagus spears. If fresh asparagus is available, by all means use it. If it is not, you will have to use either frozen or canned. Just make sure the spears are whole rather than all chopped up. Sprinkle a little paprika on top for color. Another decorating and good-tasting trick is to lay a single slice of hard-boiled egg on top of the asparagus, then sprinkle the top with paprika.

An early spring sandwich when the asparagus is young, thin, and tender.

CHEESE & ASPARAGUS

Swiss cheese, sliced
Mayonnaise
Alfalfa sprouts
Asparagus
Lemon juice
Egg bread

Lay the cheese on a slice of bread and spread it with mayonnaise. Put a light layer of sprouts on top and garnish with asparagus spears. Squeeze just a bit of lemon juice over it all.

Not exactly a quiche, but good and quick.

OPEN-FACE SANDWICH LORRAINE

(6 servings)

1 egg
3-4 strips bacon
1/3 cup cream
1 pinch nutmeg
1 pinch cayenne
1/4 teaspoon salt
1/2 pound Swiss cheese
Egg bread
Butter

Fry the bacon until crisp and drain on a paper towel. Beat the egg and add cream and seasoning. Grate the cheese and pour above mixture over it, stirring to moisten the cheese. Toast the bread, butter it, and spread with the cheese mixture. Crumble the bacon over the top and cook under the broiler for just a few moments. Watch out or the sandwiches will burn! Serve hot.

The Aesthetics of Open-Face Sandwiches

These sandwiches should be as pleasing to the eye as they are to the palate. For that reason they can often be served when a plain, closed sandwich would be inappropriate.

Because the insides of the sandwich are in this case outside, special care is required to insure a favorable response to what is seen. You must assemble an open-face sandwich thoughtfully, with a decorative eye. The order in which the ingredients are layered is as important, from a visual standpoint, as is the choice of ingredients.

Don't make the mistake of layering things on top of one another in such a way that each ingredient completely hides the one preceding it. For instance, if you were to use a large leaf of lettuce as garnish on top of the sandwich, it most likely would cover the entire thing. A visual failure and no longer open-face, the poor sandwich would lie there looking as if it was covered with a small green shroud. On the other hand, if you put that same lettuce leaf on the bottom, it would be supported by the bread and everything else would sit on top, cupped in its center with a nice fringe of green showing around the edge. There might be a large dollop of egg salad on the lettuce, with a slice of tomato on top and a little crumbled bacon. Red on yellow on green is a nice decorative combination which also tastes good.

This is not a small, long-eared, short-tailed mammal from Wales sandwich.

WELSH RABBIT
(3-4 servings)

1/4 cup beer
1/2 pound sharp Cheddar cheese,
    grated
1 egg, beaten
1 pinch cayenne
1 pinch salt
Egg bread, toasted
Paprika

Heat the beer in a double boiler, then add the grated cheese. Stir until the cheese has melted, add the beaten egg and seasoning, and continue stirring until the mixture thickens. Serve hot, spooned over toasted and buttered bread. Decorate with a sprinkle of paprika.

Here are three slightly different versions of a cream cheese sandwich.

CREAMED CREAM CHEESE & GARNISHES

Creamed cream cheese (see recipe
    page 47)
Egg bread
Crisp bacon and parsley;
    or Italian dry salami and green chile;
    or ham and parsley

Spread the bread generously with the creamed cheese and garnish with one of the combinations listed above. The bacon should be crumbled over the top. The parsley must be fresh and can be either chopped or left as a sprig. The salami should be sliced very thin and then could be cut in strips along with strips of chile, both of which you arrange on top of the creamed cheese. The chiles are not hot and can be found packed in cans, roasted and peeled. Ortega is the brand I am most familiar with. Be sure to use a good quality baked ham for your sandwiches.

Remember, the garnishes are to be used sparingly and decoratively.

Two more cheese spread possibilities.

CHEDDAR CHEESE SPREAD & GARNISHES

Potted Cheddar cheese (see recipe
    page 48)
Oat-sesame bread
Mayonnaise
Tomato and bacon;
    or chopped celery and bacon

Spread the bread with the cheese and put a dab of mayonnaise on it. Lay the slice of tomato in the mayonnaise and crumble some bacon over it.

Flash! Use cheese bread instead of cheese spread. (Makes sandwich number 3.) If you have just made a batch of cheese bread, there is a wealth of possibilities for simple, open-face sandwiches. All you need, in addition to the bread, is a little mayonnaise to spread on it and a slice of tomato and/or bacon or a couple of slices of salami or ham or practically anything else to put on top.

A fancy sandwich requiring very little effort.

CHICKEN & CANTALOUPE
(2 or 3 servings)

1/2 cup mayonnaise
1/4 teaspoon curry powder
1 1/2 teaspoons lime juice
1/2 teaspoon soy sauce

1 chicken breast
Egg bread
Butter lettuce
Cantaloupe, sliced
Lime

Mix the first group of ingredients and set aside while the flavors blend. If you have some curried mayonnaise already made (see recipe page 39), sometime try that instead of the above mixture. Poach the chicken for about 15 minutes in water to cover and slice when cool. Toast the bread and spread lightly with curried mayonnaise. Cover with a single leaf of lettuce, spread with a bit more mayonnaise. Lay the chicken on top, season with salt and pepper, and garnish with slices of cantaloupe. Squeeze a little lime juice over the top before serving.

> **Note!**
>
> Many of the closed sandwiches, straight or combination, can be made as open-face sandwiches. As you probably will notice, I have used some of the sandwiches from chapters 3 and 4 as inspiration for this chapter, but generally I have tried to provide you with sandwiches substantially different from those previously mentioned. Do not, however, let this stop you conservationists from trying to make any sandwich you want open-face and thereby saving one slice of bread. For that matter, feel free to attempt to make any open-face sandwich closed.

A post-Thanksgiving delight.

TURKEY, CREAM CHEESE & CRANBERRY

Cream cheese
Mayonnaise
Oat-sesame bread
Alfalfa sprouts
Turkey breast meat, sliced
Cranberry sauce

Soften the cream cheese by working some mayonnaise into it with a fork. Spread on the bread and cover with a layer of sprouts. Lay some thin slices of turkey on the sprouts and put a dab of good tart cranberry sauce on top. Better yet, use an uncooked cranberry relish with some orange in it.

Before you give up and dump the turkey into a soup pot, try this sandwich.

TURKEY SALAD

(2 or 3 servings)

1 cup diced turkey, white or
   dark meat
1/3 cup chopped celery
1 tablespoon lemon juice
1 pinch cayenne
1/4 teaspoon salt
1 pinch pepper
1/2 cup mayonnaise

Oat-sesame bread, toasted
Butter
Butter lettuce
Paprika
Green onion, chopped

Mix the first group. Toast and butter the bread. Lay a single leaf of lettuce on the toast and on that put a generous helping of the salad mixture. Sprinkle with a little paprika and some chopped onion.

While the ingredients are the same as the salad, this appears to be an open-face egg sandwich.

CAESAR SANDWICH

(2 servings)

1/4 cup Parmesan cheese, freshly
   grated
2 teaspoons olive oil
2 teaspoons lemon juice
1 anchovy filet
1 pinch salt
1 pinch pepper
1 pinch dry mustard

2 eggs
2 slices egg bread, toasted
Romaine lettuce

Mix the first group of ingredients into a paste. Fry the eggs, and while they are cooking, toast the bread and spread with the paste. Lay the egg on top and garnish with the lettuce cut into bite-sized pieces.

Marinated Mushrooms

1/2 pound fresh mushrooms, sliced
3 tablespoons olive oil
1 pinch rosemary
1 tablespoon lemon juice
1 small clove garlic, crushed
1/4 teaspoon salt
1 pinch pepper

Saute the sliced mushrooms in olive oil over low heat. Season with rosemary while cooking. When mushrooms are soft and tender, turn off heat, and immediately add the balance of the ingredients. Refrigerate when cool.

A good, strong dose of egg salad never hurt anyone.

EGG SALAD & GARNISHES

Herb bread
Butter
Alfalfa sprouts
Egg salad (see recipe page 53)
Marinated artichoke hearts or
    mushrooms, or chopped wal-
    nuts or anchovy filets
Paprika

Toast and butter the bread and cover with a layer of sprouts. Spoon a generous amount of egg salad on the sprouts and garnish with one of the possibilities suggested above. Sprinkle a little paprika on top.

Or. . . sprinkle a whole lot of paprika on top.

It is nice to have something like this in the refrigerator, ready for instant use.

CHICKEN LIVER PATE

1 onion, white or yellow, sliced
1/2 pound butter
1 pound chicken livers
1 tablespoon brandy
1/4 teaspoon allspice, freshly
    ground or grated
1/4 teaspoon salt
1/4 teaspoon pepper, freshly
    ground
1 hard-boiled egg
1/3 cup chopped green onion

Melt 1/2 cube butter in frying pan and saute the onion and chicken livers for 8 to 10 minutes over medium-low heat. At the last minute, add the brandy and allspice, and stir. Remove the liver and onions from the pan and put in the remaining butter to melt. Grind the liver and onions in a meat grinder or blend in a food mill or electric blender. Add the melted butter and scrapings from the frying pan. Season with salt and pepper and mix thoroughly. Chop the egg, add green onions, and mix once more, but lightly this time. Pack in a container, seal, and refrigerate. When chilled, the pate can be sliced. If it is to be spread, it will have to be brought to room temperature first.

Rye bread
Lettuce
Mayonnaise
Chicken-liver pate, sliced
Hard-boiled egg, sliced
Paprika

Simply stack up the ingredients in the order given. The garnish is a slice or two of the hard-boiled egg with a sprinkle of paprika on top.

A very simple but elegant sandwich.

SHRIMP

Small shrimp
Mayonnaise
Dill weed
Herb bread
Cucumber, sliced
Parsley

Boil the shrimp, either fresh or frozen (but fresh is best), drain and allow to cool. Mix a little dill weed in the mayonnaise and spread generously on the bread. Lay the shrimp on top and garnish with cucumber slices (leave the skin on) and parsley.

A simple but pricey little sandwich.

CRAB SALAD
(2 servings)

3-ounce package cream cheese
2 teaspoons lemon juice
2 tablespoons mayonnaise
1 pinch cayenne
1 pinch salt

1/2 cup crab meat
1/4 cup chopped celery
2 teaspoons chopped chives

Herb bread
Hard-boiled egg, sliced
Parsley

Combine the first group of ingredients. Whenever possible use fresh cooked crab, but if it is unavailable, frozen or canned crab will suffice. It will facilitate matters if the cream cheese is room temperature. Add the next 3 ingredients and mix lightly once again. Spread on herb bread and garnish with a slice of hard-boiled egg and parsley.

The preparation for this sandwich is much less involved than it looks. It is worth twice the effort.

FANCY CRAB SANDWICH

(3 servings)

1/2 avocado, mashed
1 tablespoon lemon juice
1 pinch salt
Herb bread, toasted
Butter
1 tomato, sliced
3/4 cup crab meat
1/3 cup mayonnaise
3 strips bacon, fried crisp
Parsley

Combine the first 3 ingredients and spread on buttered toast. On top, put 2 slices of tomato. Mix the crab meat and mayonnaise and spread over the tomato. Garnish with crumbled bacon and parsley.

Sprouting Alfalfa Seeds

It is possible to buy alfalfa sprouts in some grocery stores and most natural food stores. Unless a store is conveniently located and the sprouts very inexpensive, it is apt to be easier and cheaper to sprout your own. They will certainly be fresher. Seeds for sprouting are available at most natural food stores.

Put no more than 1 tablespoon of seeds in a quart jar and fill half full of lukewarm water. Cover the opening with cheesecloth or some kind of fine mesh. Soak the seeds overnight then drain, rinse, and drain again. Store them in the jar, in a dark, warm place. Put the jar on its side until the seeds have sprouted and rinse often enough to keep them from drying out. During the summer they will need to be rinsed about 3 times a day, but only once a day in winter. Always drain them thoroughly after rinsing. When the seeds have sprouted, turn the jar upside down to insure that the seeds are well-drained while they grow. When the sprouts are about 1 inch long, certainly no longer, set the jar in the sun for a few hours until they turn green. Store them in the refrigerator.

The whole sprouting and growing process should take no longer than 3 or 4 days during the summer and 5 or 6 in the winter.

A lovely, smelly sandwich.

OPEN-FACE SARDINE SANDWICH

Mayonnaise
Lemon juice
Rye bread
Alfalfa sprouts
Sardines, packed in plain oil
Red onion, sliced

Mix the mayonnaise with a little lemon juice and spread on a slice of bread. Cover with a layer of sprouts, then a layer of sardines, and garnish with a slice of red onion.

Another, slightly different, smelly sandwich.

HERRING SANDWICH

Sour cream
Oat-sesame bread
Alfalfa sprouts
Herring, pickled
Red onion, sliced

Spread a slice of bread with sour cream and cover with a layer of sprouts. Drain the herring and lay on top of the sprouts. Garnish with a slice of onion.

My favorite sandwich.

COLD SALMON

Tarragon
Mayonnaise
Herb bread
Red lettuce
Cooked salmon
Hard-boiled egg, sliced
Green onion, chopped
Lemon juice

You may use any sort of cooked salmon you want or have on hand; poached, baked, broiled, barbecued, or smoked. If I were preparing a salmon, a whole salmon, obviously, not just for sandwiches, I would cook it slowly in a covered barbecue, over smoky oak coals and hickory chips. When done, the fish should be only just cooked, very moist — never dry. The best salmon for this is the King. Being more oily than other varieties, it is less apt to dry out.

Poaching seems to be a popular way of cooking salmon. If you are primarily interested in making sandwiches and don't have a whole fish to cook, then I suppose it is about the most convenient method to use. If I sound less than enthusiastic about poaching, it is because I am very enthusiastic about barbecuing salmon. For sandwiches though, you could buy a salmon steak and broil it or get a can of smoked salmon and open it.

Crumble a bit of whole, dried tarragon with your fingers and mix it up in the mayonnaise. Set this aside for a while to give the herb flavor a chance to blend. Lay a nice big lettuce leaf on a slice of bread and spread it with the tarragon-flavored mayonnaise. Put the salmon on top and garnish with a slice of hard-boiled egg and some chopped green onion. Squeeze lemon juice over the top.

HARD-BOILED OR NOT?

Spin it. If you try to spin a hard-boiled egg on its end like a top, it will fall over, but it will spin. If it is not hard-boiled, it will simply fall over and lie there. Make the comparison. When you see the difference, you will never have to ask the question again.

Do not boil eggs longer than 10 minutes or the yolks might turn a little green around the outside. After boiling, rinse immediately in cold water.

Rolls crazy — must be raw.

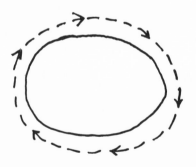

Rolls neat, stays put — must be hard-boiled.

A good way to use *el caviar cheapo*.

CAVIAR SANDWICH

(2 servings)

Egg bread, toasted
Butter
Red lettuce
Sour cream
2-ounce jar whitefish caviar
Green onion, chopped
Hard-boiled egg, sliced
Lemon juice

Lay a leaf of lettuce on each slice of buttered toast and put a good dab of sour cream on top, spreading it around just a bit. Spoon the caviar over the sour cream and garnish with some chopped green onion and a slice of hard-boiled egg. Squeeze a little lemon juice over the top.

A nice, simple dessert.

CAMEMBERT & APPLE

Camembert cheese
Pippin apple, cored and sliced
French bread

Spread a generous layer of the cheese on a thin slice of French bread, sourdough if available. Garnish with thin slices of apple.

An equally nice, simple dessert.

CAMEMBERT & PEAR

Same as above except substitute pear for apple.

Quick and delicious.

AVOCADO SLICES

Avocado
Lemon juice
Herb bread
Mayonnaise
Alfalfa sprouts
Bacon, fried crisp

Slice an avocado and squeeze lots of lemon juice over it. Spread the bread with plenty of mayonnaise and cover with sprouts. Lay the avocado slices over the sprouts and crumble the bacon over the top.

One of my favorite salads in a sandwich.

AVOCADO & GRAPEFRUIT

Grapefruit
Avocado
Egg bread
Butter lettuce
Mayonnaise
Red onion, sliced

Peel and section the grapefruit and slice the avocado. Lay a leaf of lettuce on the bread and spread it generously with mayonnaise. Lay alternate slices of avocado and sections of grapefruit in the mayonnaise and garnish with 1 or 2 thin slices of red onion.

Note! If the membrane covering the grapefruit sections is very tough, you might have to peel it off before assembling the sandwich.

A Mexican dip sandwich.

GUACAMOLE

(2 or 3 servings)

1 avocado, pitted, peeled, and
   mashed
1 tablespoon lemon juice
1 small tomato, peeled and
   chopped
1 teaspoon minced fresh cilantro
1/4 cup chopped green onions
1/4 teaspoon salt
1/4 teaspoon coarse ground
   black pepper

Herb bread
Alfalfa sprouts
Marinated artichoke hearts

     Mix the first group of ingredients to make the avo-cado spread, or guacamole. Return the pit to the bowl (to help prevent the spread from darkening), and keep covered until ready for use. Put a layer of sprouts on the bread and spread the avocado mixture into and over them very generously. Garnish with one or two quartered arti-choke hearts.

Marinated Artichoke Hearts

9-ounce package frozen artichoke
   hearts
1 pinch rosemary
3 tablespoons olive oil
1 tablespoon lemon juice
1 small clove garlic, crushed
1/4 teaspoon salt
1 pinch pepper

     Cook the artichoke hearts as in-structed on the package, but add the rosemary. When cooked, pour off liquid and immediately add the balance of the ingredients. When cool, refrigerate.

Assuming you already have the garnish, this is an easily prepared sandwich.

CHOPPED OLIVE WITH ARTICHOKE HEARTS

4 1/2-ounce can chopped olives
1/4 cup mayonnaise
Herb bread
Alfalfa sprouts
Marinated artichoke hearts (see
   recipe page 101)

Drain the chopped olives and mix with mayonnaise. Spread on herb bread and cover with a light layer of sprouts. Garnish with 1 or 2 artichoke halves.

6

Exotic Sandwiches
(Some Ethnic Approximations and Sandwiches
Which Are Cooked in a Toasting Iron)

These first two recipes are of Chinese derivation and if undertaken require an adventurous frame of mind. A willingness to try either one will be rewarded with considerable enjoyment at the table.

STIR-FRIED PORK & SMOKED OYSTERS

(serves 4)

1 small head butter lettuce
3 1/2-ounce can smoked oysters
1/2 teaspoon peeled and minced
    fresh ginger root
1/4 cup chopped green onion
1/2 cup frozen peas, thawed
3/4 pound coarse ground lean
    pork
1 tablespoon sherry
1 tablespoon soy sauce
1 teaspoon cornstarch
1 tablespoon cold water
2 tablespoons vegetable oil
1/2 teaspoon salt

Separate the lettuce leaves, wash and dry them, and store in a plastic bag in the refrigerator. They must be cold and crisp by the time you are ready to use them. Drain the oysters and mince them. Have the ground pork, ginger root, and green onion nearby but separated from each other. Make sure the peas are completely thawed. Combine the sherry and soy sauce in one small bowl and, in another, the cornstarch and water.

The mechanics of stir-frying, while a little frantic, are relatively simple. The ingredients are cooked at high heat for a short period of time, with lots of rather violent stirring and tossing about to prevent scorching. They are added to the melee separately with the order generally depending upon the difference in required cooking times. In this recipe the pork is seared in hot oil first, a little liquid is added, then the vegetables. It takes very little time to cook the ingredients compared to the time spent mincing and chopping them, but that is the secret. In order to cook quickly, everything needs to be in small minced and chopped pieces. These little pieces, when their time comes, will have to be dumped in the pan quickly, and that does not mean one at a time with thumb and forefinger, but in one fell swoop.

The stir-frying can be done in an ordinary frying pan, but it is easiest in a Chinese wok. If you use a wok, also use a Chinese spatula for stirring. It has a curved leading edge, designed to fit the rounded bottom of the wok. If you intend to stir-fry in a regular frying pan, use a large, metal kitchen spoon for stirring. Be sure the sides of the frying pan are high enough to contain all the little pieces you will be flinging about while you stir.

Remember, stir-frying takes quick action and very little time, so have everything ready. And once the cooking is done, the eating should proceed immediately.

Heat the wok or frying pan, and when it is good and hot, add the oil. Swirl it around the pan, even up the sides if you can; and when it is hot, add the salt and ginger and stir for a couple of seconds. If at any time the oil begins to smoke, or one of the ingredients looks like it is going to scorch, or even if you just want to catch your breath, simply pull the pan off the burner for a moment—but keep stirring.

Add the pork and stir-fry until it loses its pink color and some of the liquid has evaporated. Add the sherry and soy sauce and stir-fry for 1 minute. Then add the peas and chopped onion and stir-fry for 2 more minutes. Finally, add the oysters and the cornstarch and water mixture, after giving the latter a quick stir. Stir-fry for just a moment, until the oysters have mixed with the other ingredients and the cornstarch has thickened things. Remove the contents immediately to a warmed bowl and serve.

Serve it with the lettuce leaves. Spoon the mixture onto a leaf which you then roll up around it like a tortilla and eat out-of-hand.

A tea-time treat.

STEAMED, PORK-FILLED BUNS

(makes about 24)

1 1/4 cups warm water
1 tablespoon yeast
2 teaspoons sugar
2 cups unbleached white flour
1/2 teaspoon salt
2 teaspoons corn oil
2 cups unbleached white flour

Proceed per egg bread instructions on page 27, but only up to the end of the first rising, which is all this recipe requires. While the dough is rising, prepare the following ingredients for stir-frying.

1 clove garlic, minced
1/2 teaspoon peeled and minced fresh
   ginger root
1/4 cup chopped green onion
1 tablespoon sherry
1 tablespoon soy sauce
1 pound lean, ground pork
2 tablespoons vegetable oil
1/2 teaspoon salt
1 teaspoon sugar

Mince and chop those ingredients that require it, but keep them separate. Combine the sherry and soy sauce in a small bowl. If you have not already done so, read the discussion regarding stir-frying in the previous recipe.

Heat the pan and when hot, add the oil. When the oil is hot, add the salt, sugar, garlic, and ginger and stir for just a second. Add the ground pork and stir-fry until it loses its pink color and some, but not all, of the liquid evaporates. Add the sherry and soy sauce mixture and stir-fry for 1 minute. Add the onion and stir-fry for an additional minute. Transfer the mixture to a bowl to cool.

By this time the dough should have risen and after you punch it down, it will be ready for shaping into buns. On a breadboard and using your hands, roll the dough into a long cylinder about 2 inches in diameter. Cut into 1-inch sections and roll these out flat with a rolling pin

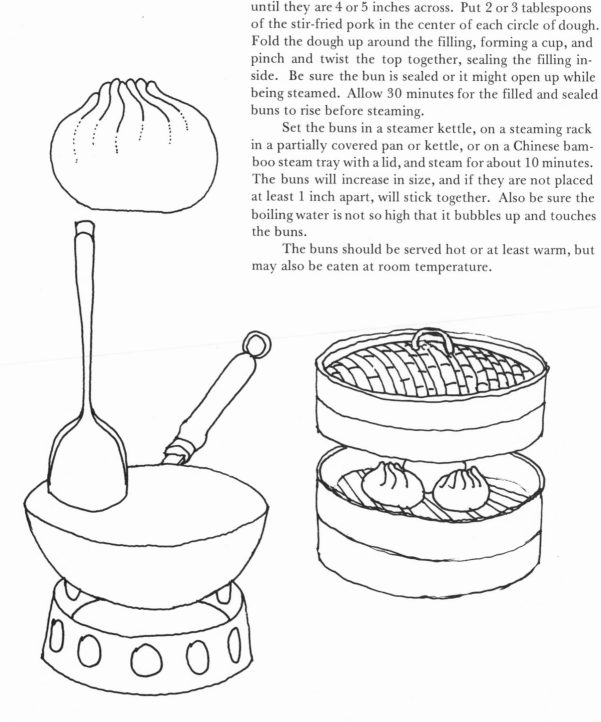

until they are 4 or 5 inches across. Put 2 or 3 tablespoons of the stir-fried pork in the center of each circle of dough. Fold the dough up around the filling, forming a cup, and pinch and twist the top together, sealing the filling inside. Be sure the bun is sealed or it might open up while being steamed. Allow 30 minutes for the filled and sealed buns to rise before steaming.

Set the buns in a steamer kettle, on a steaming rack in a partially covered pan or kettle, or on a Chinese bamboo steam tray with a lid, and steam for about 10 minutes. The buns will increase in size, and if they are not placed at least 1 inch apart, will stick together. Also be sure the boiling water is not so high that it bubbles up and touches the buns.

The buns should be served hot or at least warm, but may also be eaten at room temperature.

A rich, Middle-Eastern vegetable dish, well worth the effort involved in its preparation. It is accompanied by a very special bread.

EGGPLANT, TOMATO & CHICKPEA CASSEROLE
(4 servings)

1 cup dried chickpeas
Olive oil
1 medium-sized eggplant,
   washed but not peeled
1 large onion, sliced
1 1/2 teaspoons salt
Freshly ground black pepper
6 medium-sized tomatoes, peeled and chopped

Bring approximately a quart of water to a boil and add the chickpeas. Bring to a boil a second time and cook for 2 minutes. Turn off heat and soak for 1 hour, then drain and add fresh water to cover and bring to a boil once again. Reduce heat and simmer, partially covered, for 2 to 3 hours. Replenish water as necessary. When done, the chickpeas should be relatively tender but certainly not coming apart. Drain them and set aside.

In a large frying pan, heat enough olive oil to cover the bottom completely. While the oil is heating, cut up the eggplant. When the oil is very hot but not yet smoking, brown the eggplant cubes. This must be done as quickly as possible. Stir the cubes rapidly with a large, metal kitchen spoon to keep them from scorching. In effect, you are stir-frying, but only to brown, not to cook the eggplant completely. Replenish the olive oil as necessary and do not be surprised if a lot is used. By using the stir-frying method, you are minimizing the amount used. Put the browned eggplant in a 2-quart baking dish.

In the same frying pan, and at moderate heat, saute the onion slices in a little more olive oil. When they are tender and lightly browned, spread them in a layer on top of the eggplant and pour any oil remaining in the pan over the top. Sprinkle with about 1/2 teaspoon salt and a little freshly ground black pepper. Next put in a layer of chickpeas. Now, on top you put the peeled and chopped tomatoes — seeds, juice, and all. Sprinkle with the balance of the salt and a little more pepper.

Preheat the oven to 375 degrees and bake for about 40 minutes covered and another 10 or 20 minutes uncovered. The length of time you keep the dish covered really depends upon how moist the ingredients look. If they look runny, the dish ought to be uncovered for a longer period of time. If drying out, leave the dish covered. Allow to cool a bit before serving. This recipe should fill 10 to 12 Arabic bread halves (see recipe on page 55).

The last two ethnic approximations of sandwiches are Mexican. Happily so, I might add.

PORK TACOS

(serves 4 to 6)

3 pounds coarse ground lean
    pork
1/3 cup seedless raisins
2 cloves garlic, mashed
1/2 teaspoon salt
1/4 teaspoon pepper
1/2 teaspoon crumbled chile
    pequins
1/4 teaspoon oregano
2 tablespoons sherry
Condiments: sliced avocados,
    sour cream, chopped green
    onions
Hot sauce (see box this page)
Flour tortillas

Brown the meat quickly, a handful at a time in a stewing kettle. Set each portion aside as it is browned until it is all done; then return all of the meat to that same kettle. Add the next 8 ingredients and simmer for about 1 1/2 hours. Periodically check the liquid and replenish with small, *preheated* amounts of water if necessary. It is all right if some of the liquid evaporates, but the meat must not dry out completely. Also stir occasionally.

While the meat is simmering, prepare the condiments and put each in its own serving bowl. If you would like to make your own hot sauce, see the recipe on this page. When the meat is done and all the condiments are on the table, heat the tortillas. A few seconds on each side in a hot, dry frying pan will do the trick. As they are removed from the pan, place them in a stack, wrapped in a cloth to keep them warm. Heat only 2 per person, otherwise they will cool before they are used.

With everything set out on the table, everyone simply helps himself. Take a tortilla in hand and lay a little of the pork and each of the condiments right down the center. Roll the tortilla around everything and eat, by hand of course.

Hot Sauce for Pork Tacos

3 large tomatoes
4 green onions, chopped
2 tablespoons fresh, chopped cilantro
1 small, green, hot chile, chopped
1/2 teaspoon salt

After peeling the tomatoes, squeeze the juice into a bowl, then chop up the tomatoes and add them to the juice. Prepare and add the balance of the ingredients. Be careful when handling the chile. Do not touch your face, especially your eyes, while chopping it. For that matter, don't touch anything unnecessarily until after you have finished, cleaned up the knife and cutting board, and thoroughly washed your hands.

This hot sauce is meant to be eaten fresh. As soon as it has been prepared, it should go on the table. It will keep in the refrigerator and can also be frozen, but in neither case does it taste the same as when fresh.

A cocktail hour — or more specifically — beer hour snack.

NACHOS
(serves 2 to 4)

1 dozen corn tortillas
Vegetable oil
Salt
Refried beans (see recipe below)
1 pound Cheddar cheese, sliced
Pickled jalapeno chiles, sliced

Heat about 1/2 to 1 inch of oil in a cast-iron frying pan. A chicken fryer with high sides is best. While the oil is heating, cut the tortillas into quarters. The oil must be hot but not smoking. Deep fry the tortilla quarters, four at a time, until they stop bubbling, then just a little longer. Turn them a couple of times while frying. They should be very crisp. Set them on a paper towel to drain and salt immediately. Test one, as in *eat*, to see that they are crisp enough.

When the tortillas are done, spread them with a layer of refried beans (see recipe below), lay a slice of cheese on top, and garnish with a slice of jalapeno. Place the *nachos* on a cookie sheet and bake at 300 degrees until the cheese melts.

Here is the recipe for refried beans.

1 1/2 cups pinto beans
1 quart water
1 teaspoon salt
1 small onion, chopped
4 strips bacon

Put the beans, water, and salt in a saucepan and bring to a boil. Boil for 2 minutes then turn off heat and let the contents soak for 1 hour. Bring to a boil a second time and simmer, covered, for approximately 1 hour or until tender. Add water if necessary, but keep the water to a minimum. When the beans are tender, set them aside while you start the next step.

In a large frying pan, fry 4 strips of bacon until very crisp and set them aside to drain. Add the chopped onion to the bacon grease left in the pan and saute over low or moderate heat until tender. Crumble the bacon and re-turn to the pan with the onion and grease. Over mod-erate heat, spoon the beans into the pan and mash with a potato masher. When they are mashed and thoroughly mixed with the onion, bacon, and grease, turn off heat and remove from pan.

Don't forget the beer. Mexican beer is really fine beer, much better than ours. My favorite Mexican light beer is Superior. My favorite dark is Dos Equis.

Introducing Sandwich Toasting Irons

The sandwiches that follow are meant to be toasted in a sandwich toasting iron. This is a gadget in which a sandwich is enclosed and held over a source of heat to toast. Its most important feature is that it crimps the edges of the bread together, sealing the filling inside like a turnover. The iron has long handles for holding it over the burner of a gas or electric stove — or even a charcoal fire. When done, the sandwich is a crispy, golden brown on the outside, and the filling, sealed inside, is hot and steamy.

The French, or Croque-Monsieur, toasting iron is an attractive, cast-aluminum iron which makes two sandwiches at a time. It is available at Williams-Sonoma stores or from their mail order department: P. O. Box 3792, San Francisco, Ca. 94119. At the time of this writing they cost $12.95 plus a $1.70 shipping charge. A similar iron might be available at your local kitchen specialty shop.

The only other toasting iron I can suggest is a Toas-Tite. It is similar to the French one but is round in shape and toasts only one sandwich at a time. Evidently they are no longer made since they seem to be found only at flea markets. My wife has bought a dozen or so and has never paid more than $1.00 for them. I have seen a cheap, pressed stainless steel copy of a Toas-Tite but beware; it does not work.

Using the toasting iron is a very simple procedure. A buttered slice of bread is placed in the bottom half of the iron, buttered side down. The filling is placed on top of the bread, not all the way out to the edge but rather in the center. Be careful not to use so much filling that it keeps the sandwich from sealing. Cover with another slice of bread, buttered side up. Close the iron and toast over a burner on your stove. If the iron is cold, it will take a minute or so to warm up before the sandwich begins to toast. If it has just been used or preheated, it will only take about 1 minute on each side to toast.

We can all thank the generous people at Williams-Sonoma for the use of some of their toasted sandwich recipes.

A hot sandwich in all respects, it is both steamy and picante. A plate of these and a cold beer will either set you free or do you in.

TOASTED HAM & CHEESE WITH CHILE
(4 servings)

4 ounces cooked ham, cut into
    small pieces
4 ounces Monterey Jack or Munster
    cheese, cut into small pieces
Fresh jalapeno chile, sliced
Large green onion, chopped
Fresh cilantro
Squishy white bread*
Butter

As you cut up the ingredients, place them in separate piles on a plate. Add to this assortment a sprig of cilantro. Always remember to wash your hands thoroughly after messing around with chiles. If you forget to wash and happen to rub your eye, you will see what I mean.

Lightly butter a slice of the bread and put it buttered side down in the toasting iron. Lay some of the ham and cheese on it with a little of the onion, a slice or two of the chile, and a pinch of fresh cilantro. Cover with another slice of bread, buttered side up. Close the iron and trim off any bread sticking out around the edges. Toast over the stove for about 1 minute each side or until golden brown.

*I will have to admit, in the case of toasted sandwiches, squishy white bread is acceptable. Often the good breads seem to have too much substance, while white bread — which is mostly air anyway — becomes a thin, pastry-like shell when cooked in a toasting iron.

I took the liberty of adding cheese to this — someone else's recipe.

LA PIZZA

Bread
Butter
Tomato, sliced
Anchovy filets
Olives, sliced
Monterey Jack or Munster cheese,
    sliced

Butter the bread and lay one of the slices in the toasting iron. Remember, the buttered side is always on the outside, against the iron. Lay a thin slice of tomato in the center of the bread along with one or two anchovy filets, some of the olives, and a slice of cheese. Cover with another slice of bread, buttered side up, and toast.

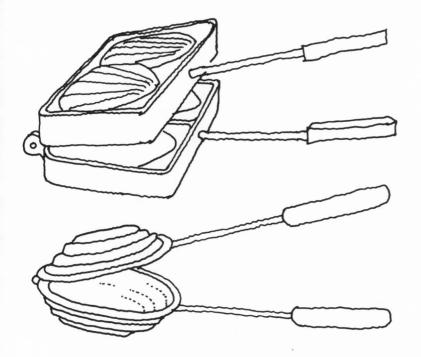

French toasting iron

Toas-Tite

**Heavy Bechamel Sauce
with Clam Juice**
(1 cup)

3 tablespoons butter
3 tablespoons flour
3/4 cup milk
1/4 cup clam juice
Salt
Pepper
1/2 bay leaf

In the top half of a double boiler, melt the butter over low heat and slowly blend in the flour. Remove the pan from the heat and put it over the hot water in the bottom of the double boiler. Slowly add the milk. Stir constantly until all the milk has been included and the sauce has become thick and smooth. Add the clam juice and seasonings.

The classic French toasted sandwich.

LE CROQUE-MONSIEUR

Bread
Butter
Gruyere cheese, sliced
Baked ham, sliced

The order of the layers is all the instruction you are going to get: Buttered bread, cheese, ham, cheese, and buttered bread.

The feminist's sandwich.

LE CROQUE-MADAME

Mushrooms, sliced
Cooked shrimp, cut into small
    pieces
Salt
Pepper
Bread
Butter
Bechamel sauce with clam
    juice (see box this page)

Saute the sliced mushrooms in a little butter and, at the last minute, add the shrimp and stir. Season to taste with salt and freshly ground black pepper. Put some of the shrimp and mushroom on the first slice of bread, spoon a little of the Bechamel sauce over the top and cover with another slice of buttered bread. Toast.

This means mushrooms.

LES CHAMPIGNONS
(2 or 3 servings)

1/2 cup sliced mushrooms
Butter
Flour
Warm water
Salt
Pepper
Egg yolk, beaten
Fresh parsley, chopped
Bread
Butter

Briefly saute the sliced mushrooms in a little butter. Combine just a little flour and water and add to the mushrooms, stirring until the mixture thickens. Turn off the heat, add the beaten egg yolk, salt, pepper, and chopped parsley, and stir a bit more. Spoon between slices of buttered bread and toast.

For the sake of ease, you may use canned ingredients, but it will taste best if you don't.

CLAMS & MUSHROOMS

Cooked clams, minced
Sauteed sliced mushrooms
Celery, chopped
Green onion, chopped
Cream cheese
Salt
Pepper
Rye bread
Butter

Prepare the ingredients and keep in separate piles on a plate. For each toasted sandwich, simply include a little of each ingredient and season to taste with salt and pepper. Slice the bread thinly and remember to butter the outside. Toast.

Another picante, toasted sandwich.

CHORIZO SAUSAGE & EGG

Egg, beaten
Chorizo sausage
Squishy white bread
Butter
Fresh jalapeno chile, sliced

Melt a little butter in a frying pan and add a bit of chorizo, mashing and stirring until it breaks up. Add the beaten egg and stir it into the chorizo, cooking only until it begins to stick together. Do not let it dry out. Place the mixture on the bare side of a buttered slice of squishy white bread and top with a slice or two of the chile. Cover with a second slice of bread buttered side up. Close the toasting iron, trim off the excess bread, and toast.

H. T. Ratatouille is back again.

SON OF H.T. RATATOUILLE & EGG

Egg, beaten
H. T. Ratatouille (see recipe
   page 67)
Salt
Pepper
Bread
Butter

Proceed as in recipe on previous page and season with salt and pepper.

Obviously there are a lot of combinations with egg and other things. Use your imagination!

The second most simple sandwich in this book.

TOASTED MINCEMEAT SANDWICH

Mincemeat, homemade or store-bought
Butter
Squishy white bread

Put a big spoonful of the mincemeat and a pat of butter between two slices of buttered-on-the-outside bread and toast.

Bananas here.

BOURDALOU A LA BANANE

Banana
Squishy white bread
Butter
Brown sugar
Rum
Apricot preserves

Cut the banana into thin, round slices. Lay the slices on the bottom slice of bread, sprinkle with a little sugar and rum, and top with a dab of the preserves. Cover with the second slice of bread, buttered on the outside.

Apples here.

LES CHAUSSONS AUX POMMES
(2 servings)

1 Pippin apple, peeled, cored,
   and sliced
1 tablespoon butter
1 tablespoon water
Cinnamon
Squishy white bread
Butter
Apricot preserves
Whipped cream

    Saute the sliced apple in the butter and water. Season lightly with cinnamon. The bread should be spread on the outside with butter and on the inside with the apricot preserves. The lightly sauteed apples go in between, of course. Toast until golden brown and serve topped with whipped cream.

And there you have it...

Since you have evidently managed to wade through this book, I hope you will now be able to set it aside and contrive to make good sandwiches of your own invention.

All I have attempted to do is send you a simple message regarding the relationship between a good sandwich and a good imagination and provide you with some examples which demonstrate that relationship.

Whenever you need a little inspiration, look through old *No Baloney* again and enjoy yourself, while you make good sandwiches.

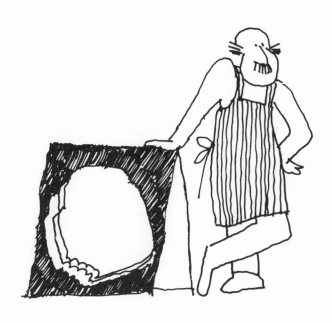

Index